Human Sexuality

A CHRISTIAN PERSPECTIVE

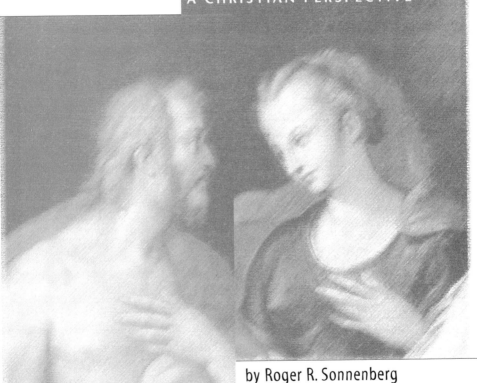

by Roger R. Sonnenberg

CONCORDIA PUBLISHING HOUSE · SAINT LOUIS

Cover design by Karol Bergdolt
Cover art by Sanmacchini Orazio, Christie's London / SuperStock
Edited by Earl Gaulke

This publication is available in braille and in large print for the visually impaired. Write to the Library for the Blind, 1333 S. Kirkwood Rd., St. Louis, MO 63122-7295; or call 1-800-433-3954.

All Scripture quotations, unless otherwise indicated, are taken from the HOLY BIBLE, NEW INTERNATIONAL VERSION®. NIV®. Copyright © 1973, 1978, 1984 by International Bible Society. Used by permission of Zondervan Publishing House. All rights reserved.

Scripture quotations marked TJB are excerpted from THE JERUSALEM BIBLE, copyright © 1966 by Darton, Longman & Todd, LTD., and Doubleday and Company, Inc. Used by permission of the publisher.

Copyright © 1998 Concordia Publishing House
3558 South Jefferson Avenue, St. Louis, MO 63118-3968
Manufactured in the United States of America

Library of Congress Cataloging-in-Publication Data
Sonnenberg, Roger.
    Human sexuality: a Christian perspective / by Roger R. Sonnenberg.
        p.   cm.   —(Learning about sex series)
    ISBN 0-570-03568-6
    Includes bibliographical references (p.   ). 1. Sex instruction. 2. Sex instruction—Religious aspects—Christianity. 3. Sex—Religious aspects—Christianity. I. Title. II. Series.
    HQ31.S668   1998
    306.7—dc 21
                                                                98-19374
                                                                CIP

5   6   7   8   9   10   11   12   13   14   18   17   16   15   14   13   12   11   10   09

This book is lovingly dedicated to

Dr. Earl Gaulke, vice-president emeritus of CPH, for his interest in and support of Christian sex education

Robin Sonnenberg, my wife of 19 years, mother and wife "par excellence," and the reason for "hallelujahs" many times and in many ways

Jacob Sonnenberg, our 10-year-old son who, after years of infertility tests, is God's gift to us, and who, because of the society we live in, knows much more about sex than I ever knew at his age

Pauline Rogers, my "right hand," my executive secretary, and Kathy Daw, my processor, who, with a great sense of humor and insight, helped me read through the manuscript and make corrections as needed

Contents

Human Sexuality:

A Christian Perspective

The Why of the Book

One needs only to go to any large bookstore to discover that there is no lack of books on sex. Titles such as *The Guide to Getting It On!* and *The Joy of Sex* titillate the appetite of even the most casual browser.

The mistake most people make is to believe that everything in these books is correct. Many of them are written with the philosophy that sex is a means to an end—sexual satisfaction, mainly your own satisfaction! Some talk about "safe sex," failing to mention there is no real "safe sex" except for abstinence until entering a monogamous marriage. Some glamorize whatever sexual identity one happens to possess. Still others are directed toward helping the readers know important secrets, such as where the famous "G Spot" is, and suggest that "if you know this important secret" you will discover ecstasy in the bedroom.

The spread of HIV/AIDS in the last decade provides the truthfulness of Hosea's words, "My people are destroyed from lack of knowledge" (Hosea 4:6). Unfortunately, the lack of knowledge about HIV has killed many physically, and even more seriously, it has killed many spiritually. How many marriages have died because some sexual addiction has enslaved one of the marriage partners?

Where do we go for knowledge? To the one who created sex, God Himself! To the one who said, "and it was very good" (Genesis 1:31). His created people were created good—without fault or defect—in physical bodies—their ears and noses, their feet and hands, their genitalia; in their ability to reproduce; in their capacity to love and be in relationship with one another.

One of the reasons for this book is to share the Creator's perspective on sex so that you might celebrate your sexuality, sex, and the making of love! Be assured, the perspective will at times be far different from the world's perspective. We should not be surprised: "For the time will come when men will not put up with sound doctrine. Instead, to suit their own desires, they will gather around them a great number of teachers to say what their itching ears want to hear" (2 Timothy 4:3).

The second reason for this book is to put into the hands of adults a book that is easily readable and understandable. Too many books are filled with the whats and the hows of sex, but not with the whys. They are written by so-called experts who are unaware of the deeper meaning of sex. They are unaware of the "divine mystery" between a man and a woman when they join together, as they experience a grand but minuscule glimpse of the "image of God" (Genesis 1:27). The book is intentionally written with language that is easy to read and understand so that readers might better appreciate their sexuality and the miraculous way God created them. As we learn how miraculous our bodies and minds are, we will most assuredly be tempted to shout "hallelujah!" We will also better know that only "the fool says in his heart, 'There is no God,'" as we examine how God has put us together so intricately to enjoy one another physically, psychologically, and spiritually (Psalm 53:1; Genesis 2:24). Some of the explanations may not be as detailed as we might like them, but in learning the basics we will have a starting point to seek additional information we might want.

As I wrote the book, I continually prayed for wisdom, knowing and believing God's promise: "If any of you lacks wisdom, he should ask God, who gives generously to all without finding fault, and it will be given to him" (James 1:5). This book is a result of that prayer and supplication. Now, my prayer is that the book will bless you in learning about your sexuality and the God-given miracle of conception and birth. As you do, may you shout your own personal "hallelujahs" and "thank You, Lord" for making all things so good!

How Much Do You Really Know about Sex?

*Mark **T** for True or **F** for False*

___ 1. Pregnancy can occur without vaginal sex.

___ 2. The use of condoms is the best way of preventing the spread of HPV (human papilloma virus).

___ 3. Sperm can live in the cervical mucus of a woman for up to five days.

___ 4. The majority of people infected by STDs know so within six months because of certain visible signs and symptoms.

___ 5. The majority of couples who cohabitate before marriage have more conflict than those who don't.

___ 6. With the exception of HIV/AIDS, most sexually transmitted diseases can now be effectively treated with drugs or surgery.

___ 7. Upon ovulation, the egg remains fertile for approximately one day.

___ 8. The egg and the sperm usually meet in the uterus.

___ 9. The average man can produce over 50 million sperm every 24 hours.

___10. Orgasm and ejaculation are the same thing for a man.

___11. The average size of an erect penis is 7.2 inches in length and 5.3 inches in circumference.

___12. Testes are only able to produce sperm when they are at a temperature higher than the temperature of the rest of the body.

___13. The average married couple spends approximately 18 minutes a week in "making love."

___14. The only purpose of physical love is procreation.

___ 15. Adam and Eve enjoyed the act of sexual intercourse before they sinned.

___ 16. Most adults masturbate.

___ 17. There is no correlation of pornography with rape.

___ 18. Semen, the fluid ejaculated through the penis, is produced in the testicles.

___ 19. A homophobic person is one who denies that homosexual behavior is moral and normal, and who opposes legal approval of such behavior.

___ 20. Research has proven that the majority of gay male relationships maintain about the same sexual fidelity as the majority of heterosexual marriage relationships.

___ 21. If a person masturbates, he/she will be more likely to develop a homosexual orientation.

___ 22. Research has shown that information and warnings about AIDS have not greatly affected sexual behavior among college students.

___ 23. Dyspareunia is a condition in which a man experiences a permanent erection, which requires medical attention.

___ 24. Arousal from taking enemas is called klismaphilia.

___ 25. A high sexual desire usually indicates that a person is sexually addicted.

Answers to "How Much Do You Really Know about Sex?"

1. *True*—Sperm can swim up the vaginal canal even without a couple having vaginal sex. Sperm have the capacity to swim long distances, making their way into the vaginal canal anytime they are deposited close to the vulva.

2. *False*—Condoms offer little protection against the spread of human papilloma virus (HPV), because the virus can be spread by cells shed anywhere around the genital area, including the scrotum area or the inner thighs of the woman.

3. *True*—Sperm can live in the cervical mucus of a woman for up to five days.

4. *False*—Studies have shown that over half of all people who are infected by STDs do not know it because of the absence of visible signs or symptoms.

5. *True*—Studies have repeatedly shown that couples who cohabitate before marriage have more conflict than those who don't cohabitate. Their communication is also poorer overall.

6. *False*—As more research is being done, it is becoming more apparent that sexually transmitted diseases often do more damage than most people realize. Some STDs are known to cause infertility. Others are known to cause serious damage to vital organs such as the brain and the heart.

7. *False*—Though an egg usually remains fertile for about 24 hours it can remain fertile for up to three days.

8. *False*—Usually the egg and the sperm meet in the fallopian tubes.

9. *True*—The average man produces 50 to 100 million sperm every 24 hours.

10. *False*—Though orgasm and ejaculation often occur together, they do not always have to. An orgasm occurs when all the muscles that tightened during sexual arousal relax and cause a pleasurable sensation to flow throughout the body. Ejaculation is when semen is released out of the body. Often an orgasm does not accompany a nocturnal emission, or ejaculation during sleep.

11. *False*—The average size of an erect penis ranges from 5 to 7 inches long and about 4.6 to 4.9 inches in circumference.

12. *False*—Testes are only able to produce sperm when they are at a lower temperature level than the temperature of the rest of the body. It is for this reason that God suspended the testes onto elastic-like cords, which move them up or down in the scrotum to help secure the correct temperature for sperm production.

13. *True*—The average married couple does spend approximately 18 minutes a week in "making love."

14. *False*—Though procreation is one of the main purposes of physical love between a husband and wife, it is not the only purpose. Passages in the Song of Songs and Proverbs clearly point out that sexual intercourse should also provide pleasure.

15. *True*—Adam and Eve enjoyed the act of sexual intercourse before they sinned. The ability to have sex was not tagged on after they had sinned as a punishment.

16. *True*—Studies show that most adults do masturbate, especially those who are single.

17. *False*—Studies show a direct correlation of pornography with rape.

18. *False*—Sperm—the male reproductive cell(s)—are produced in the testicles. Other components of semen, in which the sperm swim, are produced in the prostate gland and other internal glands and organs.

19. *False*—A person is not homophobic because he denies that homosexual behavior is moral and "normal," and therefore opposes legal

approval of such behavior. A homophobic is someone who manifests an irrational fear of homosexuality.

20. *False*— Research indicates that a very small percentage of gay male relationships are able to maintain sexual fidelity. In one study, done by a team of homosexual researchers, no homosexual couple had been able to remain faithful to each other for more than five years.

21. *False*—No research has proven that masturbation causes homosexual orientation.

22. *True*—Research has shown that all the information and warnings about AIDS have not greatly affected sexual behavior among college students.

23. *False*—When a man experiences a permanent erection it is known as priapism. The condition requires medical attention. *Dyspareunia* is a term that describes painful intercourse for women. It is similar to vaginismus.

24. *True*—A klismaphiliac does get sexually aroused by taking enemas.

25. *False*—A high sexual desire does not necessarily mean that a person is sexually addicted. One is sexually addicted only when his or her desire overshadows all other activities.

CHAPTER 1

Sexuality?
It Was God's Idea!

*So God created man in His own image, in the
image of God He created him; male and female
He created them. (Genesis 1:27)*

The phrases "sexuality," "sex," and "making
love" usually conjure up a variety of
thoughts and feelings. These thoughts and feelings are widely shaped by
the messages we receive from our parents, our grandparents, our teachers and pastors, the conversations with our friends in the locker room,
the music we listen to on the radio, the television programs we watch,
and the magazines we read. The unfortunate thing is that many of the
ideas and feelings are not always right nor are they very helpful in the
way we understand and enjoy the gift of sexuality.

Distinguishing between "Sexuality," "Sex,"
and "Making Love"

First, we must understand the difference between three often-used
phrases: "sexuality," "sex," and "making love." Unfortunately, at times
they are used synonymously as if they all mean the same thing. They
don't. Sexuality refers to our basic orientation as male or female. It
includes what we think, how we think, and why we think the way we
do—as male or female. It is not what we do, it is who we are.

Though the word *sex* can refer to one's gender, as either being male or
female, the word also means what we do as male or female. When people
talk about "having sex," they are usually referring to acting on their sexual urges by having sexual intercourse, oral sex, or anal sex with someone.
Like humans, animals have sex. "Having sex" for animals is governed by
instinct. For humans, too, there is a biological component to "having sex."

"We use a most unfortunate idiom when we say, of a lustful man prowling the streets, that he wants a woman. Strictly speaking, a woman is just what he does not want. He wants a pleasure for which a woman happens to be the necessary piece of apparatus."[1]

For the Christian, "making love" involves more than the physical act of intercourse. It includes the physical, to be sure. But it goes beyond that, to a total sharing of oneself with another person for the good of that person and for the glory of God. It is selfless. It dies to its own needs. It duplicates God's love for us—"Greater love has no one than this, that he lay down his life for his friends" (John 15:13).

In marriage, husband and wife "submit to one another out of reverence for Christ." Wives submit to their own husbands—yielding their "rights" in a relationship that grows out of Christian faith and encourages mutual love. Husbands, in a reciprocal relationship, love their wives "just as Christ loved the church and gave Himself up for her." (See Ephesians 5:21–33.)

Why We're So Confused

If we're confused about the area of sex and our sexuality, it may be because we haven't really gotten much in the way of guidance and instructions from those who have been placed over us to teach us (as commanded by Christ in Matthew 28:20). When we tried to talk to our parents, they were embarrassed, making it seem like our sexuality was shameful and bad. We may not have received useful information from our political, judicial, and educational agencies. And worse yet, the church has remained silent. Over the years, the church has, to its disgrace and shame, ignored the God-given gift of human sexuality, except to periodically shout from the pulpit "Thou shalt not."

And so where have people traditionally gone to learn about their sexuality and sex? Much of what we learn we learn indirectly through the media, secretly from our best friend after school, or through a hurry-up health class taught by our physical education teacher. We may learn the biological names and functions of our sexual organs but nothing about the all-encompassing makeup of this wonderful gift of sexuality. Because God has made us sexual human beings, we discover only too soon the natural sexual urges, but don't really know what to do with them and how to handle them in a way that is God-pleasing.

Sexuality? God's Idea from the Very Beginning

The impression is sometimes given that sexuality is one of the consequences of the fall of man into sin, making it evil and shameful. However, the opposite is true. Sexuality is really something that was part of God's original plan, something that was proclaimed as good; "God saw all that He had made, and it was very good" (Genesis 1:31). When God created people, He created them male and female, sexual human beings. In fact, our sexuality reflects the very image of God! In other words, "what we perceive as feminine and masculine characteristics are present in and derive their significance from the divine reality."[2]

Different from Animals

God created humans with the marvelous ability to have sexual union. Before they even sinned, our first parents, Adam and Eve, had sexual intercourse: "For this reason a man will leave his father and mother and be united to his wife, and they will become one flesh" (Genesis 2:24). The phrase "one flesh" indicates that they were in union physically, emotionally, and spiritually. Because they were without sin, they could openly express their love for one another; "they felt no shame" (Genesis 2:25). But how quickly sin changed this picture (see Genesis 3:10)!

It is not uncommon to hear someone lament over today's sexual promiscuity and to say, "People are acting like animals." The statement is perhaps truer than we wish to admit. Sometimes people do act like animals when it comes to their sexuality. Most animals are also born sexual. At maturity they can also reproduce through sexual intercourse. A male dog is known to break through fences if he smells a female dog in heat. In this sense, some people can behave like animals, with few morals or ethics in why they do what they do. They act on instinct or feelings instead of love.

"The magnet of sex for so many is not simply excitement, but the longing for greater closeness. And often where there has been no true intimacy in sex there is the dwindling of self-worth and self-respect when the excitement fades. That is why the loneliness which follows an encounter which is only physical can be devastating. There is much truth in the comment: 'Sex is a wonderful *symbol* of intimacy. But as we know, symbols can be empty of real meaning.' "[3]

God created humans to be far different from animals. Sexuality is more than just a means to an end. It is part of who we are. We are God's image; animals are not. We are created to be in relationship—to be in relationship first of all with the God who created us. Sadly, when humans break their relationship with God and refuse to repent, God's judgment also falls on their sexual relationships:

> *For since the creation of the world God's invisible qualities—His eternal power and divine nature—have been clearly seen, being understood from what has been made, so that men are without excuse. For although they knew God, they neither glorified Him as God nor gave thanks to Him, but their thinking became futile and their foolish hearts were darkened (Romans 1:20–21).*

> *Therefore God gave them over in the sinful desires of their hearts to sexual impurity for the degrading of their bodies with one another (Romans 1:24).*

> *Because of this, God gave them over to shameful lusts. Even their women exchanged natural relations for unnatural ones. In the same way the men also abandoned natural relations with women and were inflamed with lust for one another. Men committed indecent acts with other men, and received in themselves the due penalty for their perversion (Romans 1:26–27).*

After Adam and Eve had sinned they could no longer walk around naked. God immediately "made garments of skin" so that they might cover up their nakedness (Genesis 3:21). Why? Clifford and Joyce Penner conclude the following:

> *We believe that somehow human sexual organs and the potential they represent are symbolic of the human potential to have a relationship to*

God. Why else, when the relationship was broken, would God come and cover His creatures up?

It would seem that the total way in which two people get involved with each other in a sexual experience—the ecstatic, frantic, intense union that can occur—is a symbol of the way in which we can be intensely involved with God.[4]

A mother discovered some used prophylactics in the ashtray of her son's car. When she confronted him, he angrily said, "Mother, get with it, everyone is having sex today, including me. If God didn't want me to have sex so early, He wouldn't have put the sexual drive into me that He did."

His mother pointed to the large pet dog and said, "Son, that's what dogs and cats do that run wild. They have sex, but that's all. God created you to be different."

Tarnished by Sin

Because of the fall of man into sin, every area of human existence has been damaged, including the areas of sexuality, sex, and "making love." They lie under the domain of sin and suffer the consequences. Because of the fall, men and women became confused about their maleness and femaleness. "Making love" was replaced with "having sex." Even the joy of childbirth became hampered with "pains in childbearing" (Genesis 3:16).

The Good News is that though our first parents broke their relationship with God, God did not abandon them. God promised to send a Savior (Genesis 3:15) who would restore humans back into relationship with Him and with one another. Though Adam and Eve were expelled from the paradise garden, they were given guidance and direction on how to use the gift of sexuality; and, through a Savior, the power to act on this advice.

"Sex: The thing that takes up the least amount of time and causes the most amount of trouble."[5]

Wisdom from God on the Gift of Sexuality

Almost immediately after the fall, God started to advise His people on the use of the gift of sex. It was no different then than it is today. No other area causes more pain and emotional/social frustration than misguided sexual behavior. However, the opposite is also true. Few other things in life bring greater satisfaction and oneness than "making love" as laid out in God's Word. God not only created the drive within humans for sex, but He also set out the proper context for the complete expression and fulfillment of this drive.

Why Marriage?

Scripture gives three reasons for marriage:

1. Companionship (Genesis 2:20a–24)
2. Procreation (Genesis 1:27–28)
3. To avoid promiscuity (1 Corinthians 7:1–2)

Physical Love Is to Be Expressed between a Husband and a Wife

The Scriptures clearly teach that sexual expression of love is to be in a marriage relationship. Hebrews 13:4 proclaims that "marriage should be honored by all and the marriage bed kept pure." The word *marriage bed* in the Greek New Testament is actually *coitus*, another word for sexual intercourse. "Coitus [marriage bed] kept pure" means that the sexual union between husband and wife is not to be defiled, not soiled, not sinful.

For years, one of the leading best-sellers was a book entitled *Men Are from Mars, Women Are from Venus*, by John Gray. Though he does not write from a theological perspective, Gray states in another book, "What makes sex really great is love. The more you get to know someone and continue to grow in intimacy and love, the more the sexual experience has a chance to thrive."[6] True sexual satisfaction only takes place in a relationship where there is full and total commitment of a man and a woman in marriage for life. Though single or divorced people can talk about their "great sex life," it pales in comparison to the real thing—"a poor reflection as in a mirror" (1 Corinthians 13:12).

**How Praying Together Regularly Affects
a Couple's Sexual Satisfaction**

Wives Answered:

Prayed Regularly

    85% very happy/above average

    10% average

    5% below average

Never Pray

    73% very happy/above average

    15% average

    12% below average

Husbands Answered:

Prayed Regularly

    87% very happy/above average

    8% average

    5% below average

Never Pray

    81% very happy/above average

    5% average

    14% below average[7]

"If God meant for us to have group sex,
He'd have given us more organs."[8]

Cohabitation

Though statistics vary, all of them verify that cohabitation has increased greatly over the last 10–20 years. "What was morally reprehensible for centuries until as recently as 1970—is now the norm." The thinking among couples is that if they "try it out" before they get married, they won't have to suffer the painful consequences of divorce. However, statistics show the opposite is true. The rate of divorce for those who have cohabited and then marry is 50 percent higher than those who have not. There is also a much higher rate of violence among cohabiting couples than those who are married.[9]

"The findings are amazingly consistent; married persons, men and women, are on average considerably better off than all categories of unmarried persons in terms of happiness, sexual satisfaction, physical health, longevity and most aspects of emotional health."[10]

Physical Love Is for Pleasure

Many Christians are surprised to hear that God created man and woman with the great ability to enjoy sex, to receive pleasure from it. Pleasure was not some afterthought of God's; it was created within men and women. If not, why did He create them with the ability to have an orgasm or with body parts that would respond in surprising ways when touched by one's lover?

There is a misunderstanding among some that sex is something men enjoy and women tolerate. Studies have shown, however, that most men and women are equally motivated physically, mentally, and emotionally toward sexual cohabitation. God illustrates this truth so beautifully in His book entitled The Song of Songs: "All night long on my bed I looked for the one my heart loves" (3:1). The writer of Proverbs gives us the following wisdom, "May your fountain be blessed, and may you rejoice in the wife of your youth. A loving doe, a graceful deer—may her breasts satisfy you always, may you ever be captivated by her love" (5:18–19). He's saying it's okay to enjoy each other's bodies and to give each other pleasure through "making love."

Hindrances to a Woman's Sexual Enjoyment
The following complaints have been given by wives in response to their husbands' lovemaking.

- "He's more into physical technique than emotional intimacy."
- "He judges his lovemaking ability on the basis of whether or not he brings me to orgasm as opposed to whether or not I'm enjoying it."

- "His idea of foreplay is five minutes at the most and almost mechanical ... as if he's got a mission to perform and it's part of what he 'has to do.' He's insensitive to my needs and preferences in lovemaking."
- "Once orgasm has occurred for him or even both of us, he turns around and never touches me again for the rest of the evening."
- "He wants to make love always in the same way, the same place, the same time. ... He's lost his creativity, the spontaneity we used to have."

"There are no illegitimate children—only illegitimate parents."[11]

Physical Love Is for Procreation

God made it very clear after creating man and woman that they were to "multiply," to procreate.

So God created ... male and female ... God blessed them and said to them, "Be fruitful and increase in number; fill the earth and subdue it " (Genesis 1:27a–28).

This multiplication would take place through the act of sexual intercourse. In His infinite wisdom, God created man and woman with different parts, parts that would actually fit together, that could come together and work in such a way that they might be used by God to create new life. God could have created human beings just as He did when creating the first man—from the dust of the earth—but instead He elected to have His created beings active participants in the miracle of life.

Consistent Physical Love Is Important

God reminds us that in marriage we do not belong to ourselves alone, but to each other. As a result, we will mutually and consistently come together to share our love for one another through the act of sexual intercourse.

The husband should fulfill his marital duty to his wife, and likewise the wife to her husband. The wife's body does not belong to her alone but also to her husband. In the same way, the husband's body does not belong to him alone but also to his wife. Do not deprive each other except by mutual consent and for a time, so that you may devote yourselves to prayer. Then come together again so that Satan will not tempt you because of your lack of self-control. (1 Corinthians 7:3–5)

God is establishing some boundaries here. He's saying it's dangerous for a husband and wife to go for long periods of time without sexual activity. Satan waits for such opportunities to tempt one or both partners to go outside the marriage bed for sexual pleasure.

The question that rises is always "How long is too long?" For the man it might be one day. For the woman it might be a month. A couple must be careful not to use national averages to determine how long might be too long to abstain, but rather they should determine together, through honest communication, what is mutually satisfying and consistent enough for them both.

Sexual Activity Tidbits

A University of Chicago study discovered these interesting facts:

Those who are more highly educated have less sex than those who only finish high school (50 contacts per year for post-graduates to 58 for those who are high school graduates).

Those who work 60 hours a week or more are more sexually active than those who have more leisure time (65 contacts per year).[12]

Physical Love Requires a Time Commitment

Many women complain about a slam-bam-thank-you-ma'am attitude from their husbands regarding sexual intercourse. God says physical love requires a time commitment. He was so adamant about it that in the Old Testament He said that a newly married man should take off an entire year to "bring happiness to the wife he has married" (Deuteronomy 24:5).

Be assured, He was referring to more than sitting around under a tree and playing Monopoly. God wanted the couple to have time to enjoy each other physically, emotionally, and spiritually. It is so easy for couples to get bogged down with busy schedules and to forget to take time for one another. More than one couple has come to the therapist or pastor to say, "We're just too tired to have sex!" or "When we do have sex, it's 'let's do it quickly because we don't have much time!' "

Someone said, "If you plan to fail, you fail to plan." A wise couple will make plans for weekend escapes, or a night away at a local hotel, or some regular times each month to enjoy one another sexually.

A Picture of the Difference between "Having Sex" and "Making Love"

As we've noted, there's a difference between "having sex" and "making love." In 1 Corinthians 13, Paul was writing that church members must temper their relationships with love. His words also serve as a vivid picture of what marital love should be. If love is not present in a marriage, then "having sex" is like "a resounding gong or a clanging cymbal" (v. 1). Have you ever had to put up with "a clanging cymbal" for very long? It can drive you crazy after a while. St. Paul goes on to say that one can speak in the most beautiful way, one can "have the gift of prophecy and can fathom all mysteries and all knowledge," one can "have a faith that can move mountains," but without love all these things are useless (v. 2). Yes, the greatest sex without love is nothing. It is simply two people using one another.

A celebration of love through sexual intercourse is marked by the very things St. Paul talks about in verses 4 through 8:

> *Love is patient, love is kind. It does not envy, it does not boast, it is not proud. It is not rude, it is not self-seeking, it is not easily angered, it keeps no record of wrongs. Love does not delight in evil but rejoices with the truth. It always protects, always trusts, always hopes, always perseveres. Love never fails.*

The love described is "agape [ah-GAHP-ay] love," God-given love. It is what the love of God looks like. It is what God wants married love to look like. When it does, then two come together, not to "have sex," but to "make love."

CHAPTER 2   Gender and Sexual Orientation

Even their women exchanged natural relations for unnatural ones. In the same way the men also abandoned natural relations with women and were inflamed with lust for one another."
(Romans 1:26–27)

Few areas of sexuality are more debated and talked about today than the area of sexual orientation. Sexual orientation refers to the gender to which a person is emotionally and physically attracted. The following terms are used to describe the sexual orientation of people:

Sexual Orientation

Orientation	Name
Sexually attracted to the opposite sex	Heterosexual (straight)
Sexually attracted to the same sex	Homosexual (gay for men, lesbians for women)
Sexually attracted to both sexes	Bisexual

Homosexuality

Homosexuality is the term used to describe a sexual orientation toward someone of the same sex. The term comes from the Greek word *homo*, which means "the same." There are other names used to describe this same orientation, such as *gay* for men and *lesbian* for women.

Ways Homosexuals Express Sexual Desire
Mutual Masturbation (including anal-finger manipulation)
Oral Copulation—insertion of the penis into partner's mouth
Anal Copulation—insertion of the penis into partner's rectum
Anal/Oral Sex (rimming)—licking/insertion of the tongue into
    partner's rectum
Vaginal/Oral Sex—licking/insertion of the tongue into
    partner's vagina[1]

The "Why" of Homosexuality

Scientists have debated for years about whether or not gender orientation is biologically or environmentally determined. In recent years some have suggested that homosexuality is a genetic predisposition. However, the consensus seems to be that all sexual orientation, including homosexuality, is too complicated to be solely attributed either to biology or to environment.

A self-avowed homosexual, Dr. Simon LeVay of the Salk Institute in San Diego, California, suggested that his research showed that autopsies of the brain structure of homosexuals differed from those of heterosexuals. The media immediately latched onto the story and announced that LeVay's research proved conclusively that sexual orientation was genetically determined. However, LeVay's research has been repeatedly challenged. According to the *Los Angeles Times*, neuroscientist and psychologist Marc Breedlove of the University of California at Berkeley has "produced evidence from laboratory studies on rats which suggests that sexual behavior changes the human brain, not vice versa."[2]

Biological essentialists believe homosexuality is inborn, established at birth due to genetic and hormonal factors. This thinking suggests that though homosexuals may have an option as far as their sexual activity, they have no choice as far as their erotic and emotional attraction. Some of the research that has featured this philosophy has been done by homosexuals themselves in an attempt to rationalize their behavior. In discussing this philosophy and the research supporting it, Ed Young, in his book, *Pure Sex*, observes:

"When a 1993 study in Science suggested the link between genetics and homosexuality, the media readily seized on the story with enthusiasm. ... Easily ignored amid the hype was a brief quote from a noted geneticist who expressed reservations, saying the incidence of the Xq28 gene among homosexual men might well be associational, not causal."[3]

The American Psychiatric Association has adopted much of the thinking that our sexual orientation is determined genetically. In 1952 the APA placed homosexuality among the sociopathic personality disturbances that needed treatment. In 1968, however, the APA removed homosexuality from their Diagnostic and Statistical Manual of Mental Disorders (DSM). They simply stated that homosexuality is only a problem when it is incompatible with the person's sense of self. This means that when a person is comfortable with his or her thoughts and feelings about homosexuality, it is not a disorder that needs to be dealt with by counselors.

Social constructionists believe that homosexuality is due mainly to environmental and social factors. Joseph Nicolosi, founder and director of the Thomas Aquinas Psychological Clinic in Los Angeles, California writes:

In reality, the homosexual condition is a developmental problem—and one that often results from early problems between father and son. A heterosexual development necessitates the support and cooperation of both parents as the boy disidentifies from mother and identifies with father. Failure in relationship with father may result in failure to internalize male gender-identity. A large proportion of the men seen in psychotherapy for treatment of homosexuality fit this developmental syndrome. ... Failure to fully gender-identify results in an alienation not only from father, but from male peers in childhood.[4]

In counseling homosexuals, therapists often discover that there is an absence of affection or a distancing from a parent of the same sex. Feeling this absence, it has been suggested that homosexuality is an attempt to "repair" that deficit. For example, when a homosexual meets another man who is what he would like to be, but thinks he isn't, he idealizes him and is attracted to him. Needless to say, not everyone agrees with this thinking.

The Number of Homosexuals

For years we were taught that approximately 10 percent of the population is homosexual. This statistic came out of a study done by Alfred Kinsey, who began his research in the '30s and '40s. Though the scientific world accepted his findings, they did not study how he arrived at this figure. His polling was skewed in that he asked for volunteers and got them, many from prisons and reform schools. It's reported that homosexuals actually recruited other homosexuals to be a part of the study.

In the last few years, more accurate research has been done and has found that the percentage of homosexuality is much lower than Kinsey reported. Though some of the statistics vary, the consensus is that around 2 to 3 percent are sexually attracted to the same sex. Some of the most recent research, as reported in *Sex in America*, states thus:

> *About 5.5 percent of the women said they found the thought of having sex with someone of the same gender very appealing or appealing. About 4 percent of the women said they were sexually attracted to individuals of the same gender ... About 6 percent of the men in our study said they were attracted to other men. About 2 percent of the men in our study said they had sex with a man in the past year, a little more than 5 percent said they had homosexual sex at least once since they turned eighteen, and 9 percent said they had had sex with a man at least once since puberty.*[5]

The "Gayness" of Homosexuality

Though *gay* is a word used to describe homosexuality, homosexuals often have a less-than-happy time in society. Despite television programs that suggest that homosexuality is simply an alternate lifestyle, homosexuality, though tolerated, is not viewed as an acceptable sexual orientation by many. There is still great opposition and prejudice against homosexuals in most workplaces and most communities. Sexual activity between same-sex couples is still against the law in some states.

Although most heterosexuals desire to be in a relationship with another person for a lifetime, research has proven that among homosexuals, lifetime fidelity is rarely the case. For example, one study indicated that 28 percent of homosexual males have 1,000 or more partners. Their promiscuity indicates anything but "gayness." Another study was done by a homosexual couple in an attempt to disprove the contention that gay male relationships do not last.

After much searching they were able to locate 156 male couples in relationships that had lasted from 1 to 37 years. Two-thirds of the respondents had entered the relationship with either the implicit or the explicit expectation of sexual fidelity.

The results show that of those 156 couples, only seven had been able to maintain sexual fidelity. Furthermore, of those seven couples, none had been together more than five years. In other words, the researchers were unable to find a single male couple that was able to maintain sexual fidelity for more than five years.[6]

Research has shown that one of the elements found in people who claim to be happy is that they are in meaningful relationships with other people. Though many homosexuals claim they have close relationships with others, the promiscuity of many would indicate a deep and inner searching for much more. For a relationship to be meaningful, it must be more than sexual.

By its very nature, the sex act between two people of the same gender cannot provide the fulfillment that the sex act between two people of the opposite sex can. Though two homosexuals are in the company of one another as the sex act is going on, the act itself is still isolated and narcissistic. It is experienced separately.[7] There is no mutual, "one flesh" experience (Genesis 2:24).

Homophobia is the fear and hatred of homosexuals. Though the term is sometimes used to describe people who oppose legislation protecting homosexual behavior and who believe that homosexual behavior is contrary to God's will, homophobia is irrational fear, to the extent that one may want to even do physical harm to homosexuals. A homophobic person may even believe that homosexuality is contagious, like catching the common cold. Homophobic people need professional help just as anyone who has any irrational fears.

But What Does the Bible Say?

The Christian cannot judge homosexuality on the basis of research or expert opinions. Rather, homosexuality must be looked at in the light of Scripture. Though some Christians believe that many of the statements made in Scripture about homosexuality are open to a wide range of interpretation, most would agree that the Bible states clearly that the practice of homosexual behavior is outside of God's will and is sinful. Some of these passages include Genesis 19:1–13; Leviticus 18:22; 20:13; Judges 19:22–30; Romans 1:21–27; 1 Corinthians 6:9–11; 1 Timothy 1:9–11; 2 Peter 2:6–10; and Jude 7.

Some theologians have stated that the sin that brought about Sodom and Gomorrah's destruction was one of inhospitality, not sexual perversion. However, it is clear from Genesis 19:5 that sodomy and anal sex with men was one of the chief sins responsible for the downfall of Sodom and Gomorrah. Jude 7 further reiterates this truth: "In a similar way, Sodom and Gomorrah and the surrounding towns gave themselves up to sexual immorality and perversion. They serve as an example of those who suffer the punishment of eternal fire."

Still others say that what St. Paul was talking about in Romans 1:21–27 was the sin of promiscuity, not the sinful behavior of two males or females in an ongoing sexual relationship with one another. Though promiscuity is sinful, there is no reference to that being the sin St. Paul speaks of. Because people willingly turned away from God, God "gave them over to shameful lusts" (v. 26). The text goes on to describe homosexual behavior as an example of what is meant by "shameful lusts": "Even their women exchanged natural relations for unnatural ones. In the same way the men also abandoned natural relations with women and were inflamed with lust for one another. Men committed indecent acts with other men, and received in themselves the due penalty for their perversion" (vv. 26–27).

Despite attempts at disproving the validity of certain passages in Scripture that speak against homosexual behavior, a careful look at the passages can't help but make one conclude that living a homosexual lifestyle is wrong. Though some would say it is merely an alternative lifestyle—one that needs to be accepted by all—the Christian would have to say it is not a lifestyle pleasing to God.

"Do you not know that the wicked will not inherit the kingdom of God? Do not be deceived: Neither the sexually immoral nor idolaters nor adulterers nor male prostitutes nor homosexual offenders nor thieves nor the greedy nor drunkards nor slanderers nor swindlers will inherit the kingdom of God. And that is what some of you were. But you were washed, you were sanctified, you were justified in the name of the Lord Jesus Christ and by the Spirit of our God" (1 Corinthians 6:9–11).

But Can Homosexuals Change?

There are few myths more dangerous today than the one that says homosexuals are the way they are, and, even if they want to change, they can't. Wrong! Though it is not easy to alter one's desires or behavior, it can be done with God's help. If not, everything God says about the empowerment He gives us through the new life we have in Jesus Christ is false.

I pray ... that the eyes of your heart may be enlightened in order that you may know ... His incomparably great power for us who believe. That power is like the working of His mighty strength, which He exerted in Christ when He raised Him from the dead and seated Him at His right hand in the heavenly realms. (Ephesians 1:18, 19–20)

When Scripture says we have the power that raised Christ from the dead, it is saying that we are not powerless against any sin. We are armed with the power of the God who created us, who raised Christ back to life, who changed us from sinner to saint.

This is not to say that change is easy. It isn't. It requires confession and healing. It requires the help of others—therapists, counselors, pastors, and family. Even secular researchers such as Masters and Johnson have reported great success with sexual reorientation. Christian organizations such as Exodus International and Love in Action are available to help those who seek to get out of a homosexual lifestyle.

Though sexual attraction may not be chosen, sexual behavior is!

Bisexuality

The term *bisexual* refers to people who are sexually attracted to both genders. The Latin preface *bi* means "two." Sigmund Freud suggested that we are all inherently bisexual and that we simply choose not to act on it. In recent years, bisexuality has received a lot of attention. A major magazine actually carried a story calling it the "new sexual identity."

The practice of bisexuality is more common among women than men. Men are more attracted by seeing two women together. Because of this, many of the popular "skin" magazines for men feature two women having sex together. However, the majority of women do not necessarily enjoy seeing two men having sex together.

Bisexual behavior is the same as homosexual behavior in God's eyes. Despite what Freud or any other so-called experts might say, bisexuality is "unnatural." In His creative plan, God gave male and female separate organs and parts to function in relationship with a member of the opposite sex. No matter how one looks at it, bisexuality can never culminate into a total "one-flesh" experience.

Woman was created to meet the needs of man, and also in such a way that man would meet her needs. Either without the other is incomplete. The key and lock as one mechanism and the violin and bow as one instrument ... they can make sweet music together—together they are a complete musical instrument.[8]

Cross-Dressing

Some men and women experiment with gender roles by dressing up in clothing that is worn by members of the opposite sex. A few may actually make a career of cross-dressing. Men who are cross-dressers are referred to as "drag queens." Women who dress up like men are called "drag kings."

Those who cross-dress for sexual gratification are referred to as "transvestites." In contrast, transsexuals fully identify with the gender they dress in and inwardly desire to be that gender biologically as well. Some will even use hormone therapy and go through surgery to anatomically change their sex.

Gender Confusion

St. Paul says that such gender confusion is one of the consequences of people wilfully forgetting their Creator—God. When people reject God, they become confused about who they are, and about their relationship with others. "Their thinking became futile and their foolish hearts were darkened" (Romans 1:21).

However, Jesus is still Lord! He triumphed over any confusion and sexual problems with His life, death, and resurrection, and empowers us to do the same.

Where sin increased, grace increased all the more, so that, just as sin reigned in death, so also grace might reign through righteousness to bring eternal life through Jesus Christ our Lord. (Romans 5:20–21)

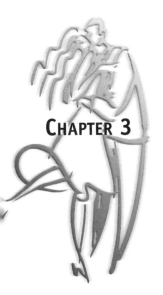

CHAPTER 3

The Bodies We Have

For You created my inmost being; You knit me together in my mother's womb. I praise You because I am fearfully and wonderfully made; Your works are wonderful. (Psalm 139:13–14)

Nothing God created matches His last creation—the creation of man and woman. Yet, this miraculous creation is described in the simplest of ways:

Then God said, "Let Us make man in Our image, in Our likeness, and let them rule over the fish of the sea and the birds of the air, over the livestock, over all the earth, and over all the creatures that move along the ground." So God created man in His own image, in the image of God He created him; male and female he created them. (Genesis 1:26–27)

Everything about man was good—fingernails, toes, eyebrows, teeth, arms, scrotum, penis, testicles. Everything about woman was good—fingernails, toes, eyebrows, teeth, arms, vulva, clitoris, vagina. To each He gave what they needed for life. God designed each man and woman with special internal and external sex and reproductive organs. These organs are called *genitalia*, a word coming from the same root word as *genesis*. Genitalia means "to give birth."

These organs, however, were also created to bring pleasure to man and woman. Most boys and girls discover this at an early age. Boys may discover this sooner than girls because from early on they need to hold on to their penis five to seven times a day in order to go to the bathroom. Thus, they become familiar with the feel of their organ. They will play games with it, doing such things as aiming it while urinating, to see if they can hit some other object floating in the toilet. More than one mom has asked what to say after discovering little Denis playing with his penis while taking a bath and exclaiming, "Look, Mommy, it gets bigger when I rub it."

The Sexual Anatomy of a Woman

In creating the world and all that was in it, the Scriptures announced, "God saw all that He had made, and it was very good" (Genesis 1:31). Most men would exclaim of His last creation—the creation of woman—"Yes, it is very good." The story of how He did it is put simply like this:

> So the LORD God caused the man to fall into a deep sleep; and while he was sleeping, He took one of the man's ribs and closed up the place with flesh. Then the LORD God made a woman from the rib He had taken out of the man, and He brought her to the man. The man said, "This is now bone of my bones and flesh of my flesh; she shall be called 'woman,' for she was taken out of man." (Genesis 2:21–23)

As Solomon looked upon his wife he exclaimed, "How beautiful you are, my darling! Oh, how beautiful!" (Song of Songs 4:1). He saw her as beautiful—physically, emotionally, and spiritually.

> "Men go abroad to wonder at the height of mountains, at the huge waves of the sea, at the long courses of the rivers, at the vast compass of the ocean, at the circular motion of the stars; and they pass by themselves without wondering." *St. Augustine*

The Outside Organs

A woman's outside genital is called the *vulva*, from the Latin word meaning "covering." Some believe that Solomon was describing the vulva as his wife danced naked before him: "Your navel is a rounded goblet that never lacks blended wine" (Song of Songs 7:2). The word translated *navel* can also read be read as *vulva*. The use of the word "vulva" makes more sense in the context. Solomon's wife is dancing naked before him. He begins to describe her beauty beginning at her feet and moves on up her body. The "rounded goblet" refers to a bowl. It contains blended wine, wine that he said he drank of earlier: "I have come into my garden, my sister, my bride; I have gathered my myrrh with my spice. I have eaten my honeycomb and my honey; I have drunk my wine and my milk" (Song of Songs 5:1).

The vulva consists of these parts (see diagram):

- the mons pubis covered by pubic hair
- the major lips (labia majora)
- the minor lips (labia minora)
- the urethra
- the vaginal opening
- the clitoris tip or head

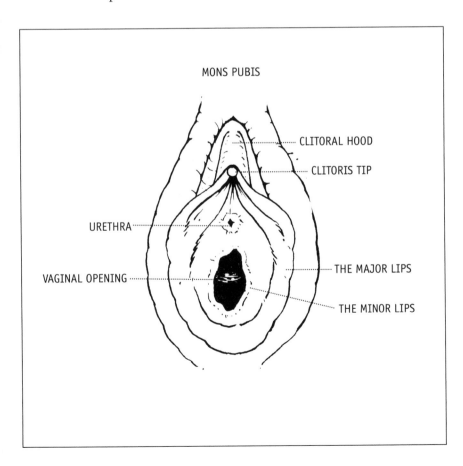

MONS PUBIS

CLITORAL HOOD

CLITORIS TIP

URETHRA

VAGINAL OPENING

THE MAJOR LIPS

THE MINOR LIPS

The Mons

The most visible part of the vulva is the fatty tissue above the sex organs on the pubic bone. Upon puberty, hair grows and covers most of this area. The hair is usually in the shape of a triangular pattern. This area is often neglected in lovemaking—unfortunately so, because it is an area that is very sensitive to touch and excitable due to the many nerve endings located in it.

The Major Lips (Labia Majora)

The two folds between the woman's legs are known as the *major lips (labia majora)*. The size and shape of these folds vary with different women. During puberty they usually become darker in color and the outer edges may be covered with hair. These outer lips cover the vaginal opening.

The Small Lips (Labia Minora)

The two parallel folds of skin that connect as a hood over the clitoris are known as the *labia minora* or *small lips*. The stimulation and arousal of these lips during intercourse can also arouse the clitoris. During arousal the lips will enlarge.

The Urethra

The urethra is the tube that opens below the clitoris and above the vaginal opening. The primary function of the urethra is as a passage for urine. There is some evidence that during sexual intercourse and orgasm, a clear ejaculatory fluid shoots out of the urethra in approximately 10 percent of women. Some experts claim, however, that this fluid is nothing more than urine pressed out of the bladder due to orgasm.

The Vaginal Opening

The vaginal opening is located under the urethral opening. The vagina itself is a muscular tube that connects the woman's external sexual organs with her internal ones. It is a main center of sexual arousal, receives the male penis when having sexual intercourse, and serves as a canal to usher a newborn baby into the world. Unless something is inserted into the vagina the muscles are collapsed, much like a deflated balloon. About four inches deep before arousal, it can deepen much more during sexual arousal. The elasticity of the vagina is obvious in that it can stretch enough to allow a baby to pass through. Upon sexual arousal the outermost part of the vagina becomes narrower while the part closest to the cervix expands.

At birth a thin membrane of skin called the *hymen* usually covers the opening of the vagina. The size and the shape of the hymen varies in women. In some women it may completely cover the opening of the vagina. In still others it may be more web-like. Most hymens have one or more openings in order to allow for menstrual flow to pass out of the body.

There is some indication that there is a small area in the vagina that is more sensitive during intercourse than the rest of its tissue. It was discovered by the German physician Grafenberg; thus, they named the spot the "G spot." His research indicated that it was located several inches inside the vaginal opening and that during sexual play the spot swells and intensifies sexual pleasure.

> "The clitoris is unique in that it is the only organ in human anatomy whose purpose is exclusively that of erotic excitation and release."[1]

The Clitoris

Just as the penis in a male is extended during arousal, so is a small organ in the woman called the *clitoris*. The word *clitoris* literally means "that which is closed in." It is closed in by other parts of the vulva, specifically the major and minor lips. The shaft of the clitoris is approximately an inch long and is located about an inch from the vagina. The most obvious part of the clitoris is a small pea-shaped tip called the glans. Covering the tip is a hood called the prepuce.

As the woman is sexually aroused, her clitoris swells. Because the clitoris is often not directly stimulated by the thrusting of the penis, some women desire additional stimulation of the clitoris by pressing it against the man's pubic bone during sexual intercourse.

Throughout Europe and the United States, fearing the "dangers of masturbation," it was not uncommon for doctors to surgically remove the woman's clitoris. The procedure was known as a "clitoridectomy." In doing so, they thought it would discourage girls from masturbating, thus, keeping them from going insane! The surgery is still widely done in many African and Asian cultures. In some cultures clitoridectomies are done for religious reasons or as a rite of passage into adulthood.

Female Circumcision

Female circumcision is practiced by some Islamic conservatives, though recently the highest court of Egypt ruled that there was nothing in the Koran that permitted or sanctioned such an act. Female circumcision is the removal of a girl's clitoris, as well as some of the outer genital area, in order to strip her of sexual feelings. The procedure is often carried out by traditional practitioners or family members using simple knives or razor blades, causing some of the girls to bleed to death during or after the surgery. Others come down with serious infections.

Breasts

When considering a woman's anatomy, we must not forget one of the most miraculous aspects of a woman's body—her breasts. Solomon poetically described them as "two fawns, like twin fawns of a gazelle that browse among the lilies" (Song of Songs 4:5). The main purpose of breasts is to nurture new life by producing milk for a baby. They contain clusters of milk glands that upon the birth of a child begin a process called lactation, the production of milk. Milk ducts bring this milk to the nipple, where it is drawn out by a baby's sucking. The area surrounding the nipple of a woman's breast is called the areola. The area varies in size and color, though usually it is much darker than the rest of the breast.

Breasts are some of the most erogenous areas on a woman's body. Many women report that stimulation of the breasts provides sexual pleasure. The degree of pleasure can often depend on the time and stage of her menstrual cycle.

Breasts are different sizes. God didn't create different sizes to amuse

His people or to embarrass them. He may have simply created different sizes as a counterpart to the differing likes of different men. Some men are sexually attracted to women with large breasts, and still others prefer women with smaller ones.

Unfortunately our society has over-emphasized the importance of breast size, just as it has with the size of a male's penis. Our culture has come to believe that larger is better, more sexy, more desirable. Such thinking has led women to seek breast enlargements, even though many of the techniques and devices used have proven to be unsafe.

Mammogram

Physicians recommend that women have regular breast examinations, especially after a woman turns 40. The physician will look for any anomalies or anything that is out of the ordinary, such as a lump. A mammogram, which should also be had regularly, is a sensitive X-ray procedure used to discover small breast tumors. Though many women fear the worst when a lump or tumor is detected, it does not necessarily mean it is cancerous.

The Inside Organs

Unlike the male, most of the female genitalia are tucked inside her body. These organs consist of two ovaries, two uterine or fallopian tubes, the uterus or womb, and the greater part of the vagina (see diagram).

The Ovaries and the Menstrual Cycle

The ovaries, approximately the size of large almonds, are located one on each side of the uterus. They are directly behind and below the fallopian tubes. The word *ovary* comes from the Latin *ovum*, egg. It is in the ovaries where eggs or ova are produced each month. It is also a place where the sex hormones are produced that affect the menstrual system. Fourteen to fifteen days before menstruation, one ovary releases an egg into a fallopian tube where it is carried by finger-like fringes *(fimbria)* located in the oviduct and carried to the uterus to await a union with the sperm. The egg's journey is miraculous to say the least since the oviduct is not attached to the ovary (note the diagram). If the ovum does not become fertilized it is discharged from the body during the time of menstruation.

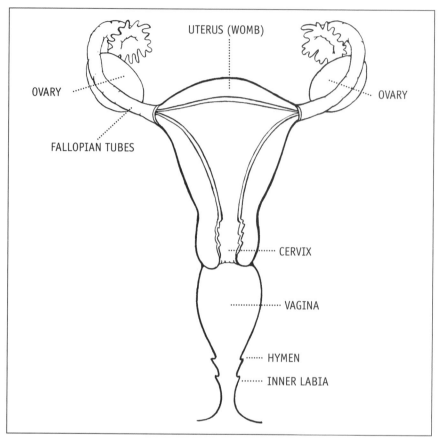

Menstruation is God's way of preparing the womb each month for the possibility of new life through pregnancy. However, experts have also noted that menstruation is God's way of getting rid of bacteria and other microbes brought into the body through sexual intercourse. The blood vessels in and through the endometrium (topmost layer of skin in the uterus) contain immune cells that kill the germs.

Long before the experts suggested that this was one of the functions of menstruation, God had already alluded to it in Scripture. He used the bodily function of menstruation as a way of talking to us about the need for forgiveness and cleansing; "When a woman has her regular flow of blood, the impurity of her monthly period will last seven days, and anyone who touches her will be unclean till evening" (Leviticus 15:19). It was not that those touching anything the woman touched would necessarily become physically sick but simply that her monthly menstruation symbolized the spiritual sickness of all mankind brought about by sin. The discharge of that which was impure in the body symbolized the need to get rid of that which makes us unholy—sin. Atonement was needed. In order to do this, a woman who was going through menstruation was required to bring two doves or pigeons to the priest. The priest would sacrifice one for a sin offering and the other for a burnt offering. "In this way he will make atonement for her before the LORD for the uncleanness of her discharge" (Leviticus 15:30).

The procedure described in the Old Testament was a foreshadowing of the atonement that would come through Jesus Christ. Sin separates all people from a holy God. The result? Death. However, atonement was made for mankind through the life, death, and resurrection of God's Son, Jesus Christ.

Jesus demonstrated the old way of making atonement with the new that came with Him, through the story of the woman who was subject to an abnormal menstrual flow for twelve years (Mark 5:24–34). A woman struggled to reach out from among the crowd to touch the garment of Jesus as He walked by her. She knew that the medical doctors could not do for her Jesus could. Normally, any person having contact with her during this flow of blood would have been considered unclean under the Old Covenant (Leviticus 15:25–33). Jesus demonstrated things were now different. With a mere touch, Jesus' power left Him and restored the woman to health (Mark 5:30).

Menstrual—from the Latin word *mensis*, which means "month." At approximate monthly intervals, a woman sheds the endometrium—the thin lining of the uterus—unless pregnancy occurs.

The Preovulatory Phase

The growth of an egg (ovum) takes place in one of the ovarian follicles. The endometrium, the inner lining of the uterus, begins to grow with the enlargement of blood vessels and glands. Both occur because the pituitary gland is secreting a follicle-stimulating hormone (FSH). This hormone persuades the ovaries to "ripen" one or more of the eggs and to produce estrogen. Estrogen, produced by the ovaries, in turn tells the uterus to get ready for possible pregnancy.

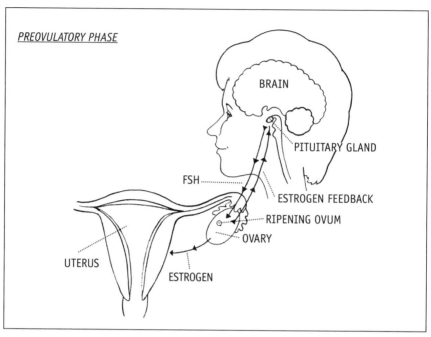

PREOVULATORY PHASE

BRAIN

PITUITARY GLAND

FSH

ESTROGEN FEEDBACK

RIPENING OVUM

OVARY

UTERUS

ESTROGEN

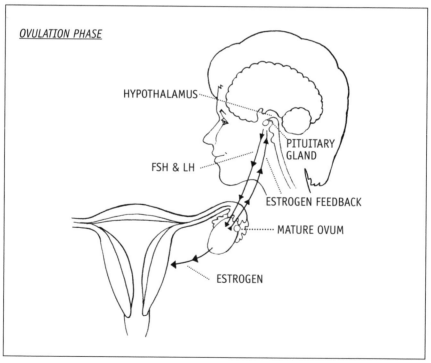

OVULATION PHASE

HYPOTHALAMUS

PITUITARY GLAND

FSH & LH

ESTROGEN FEEDBACK

MATURE OVUM

ESTROGEN

The Ovulation Phase

With the buildup of estrogen, the hypothalamus of the pituitary gland triggers the release of a hormone that in turn triggers ovulation, or the release of the egg from the ovary to the fallopian tube. During this period, studies have shown that a woman often experiences a stronger than normal desire for sex.

The Luteal Secretion Phase

The same luteinizing hormone (LH) from the pituitary gland that caused ovulation also causes the ovaries to produce another hormone called *progesterone*. This hormone triggers the uterus to get ready for possible pregnancy by thickening the uterine lining. While the bed is being made in the uterus, the ovum takes its time, approximately three to four days, journeying through a fallopian tube to the uterus. The long journey gives the egg a greater opportunity to meet with a speeding sperm in hopes of fertilization. If fertilization is to occur, it must happen here, in a fallopian tube. If fertilization doesn't occur, the ovum dies.

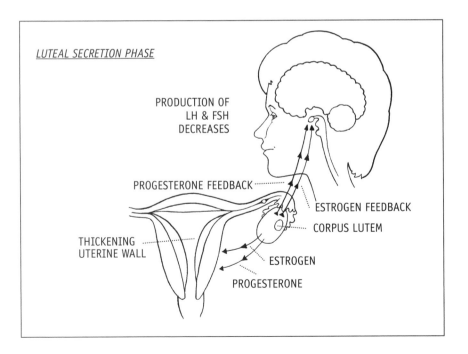

Premenstrual Syndrome (PMS)

Prior to menstruation, a woman can experience varying mood swings, such as crying spells and nervousness. Often she also has certain physical symptoms, such as abdominal bloating and tenderness in the breasts. Difficulties during this seven-day period after ovulation and prior to menstruation is known as "premenstrual syndrome," or what is commonly known as "PMS."

The Menstruation Phase

If there is no pregnancy, the endometrium, the inner lining of the uterus, breaks down, dislodges from the uterus, and passes out through the vagina. Just a few days previous, the endometrium had consisted of thousands of small blood vessels and millions of lively cells of sponge-like tissue. If pregnancy had occurred, the endometrium would have fed the embryo, daily softening the bed for the new life to lie in. However, when a fertilized egg does not show up, the hormone stops supplying the endometrium with the necessary stimulation and ingredients for life. The blood vessels shrink, causing the lining to loosen, detach from the uterus, and to flow out of the vagina.

The Menstrual Cycle

- The menstrual cycle from beginning to end is between 26 and 32 days.
- Most women menstruate for approximately four to five days.
- The amount of menstrual flow varies with women; however, for most women it is approximately five to six tablespoonsful of liquid.
- The process of menstruation begins at puberty and continues until menopause. The first time of menstruation, called the *menarche*, begins between ages 9 to 16. When menstruation ceases, called *menopause*, a woman is typically between the ages of 45 and 55.

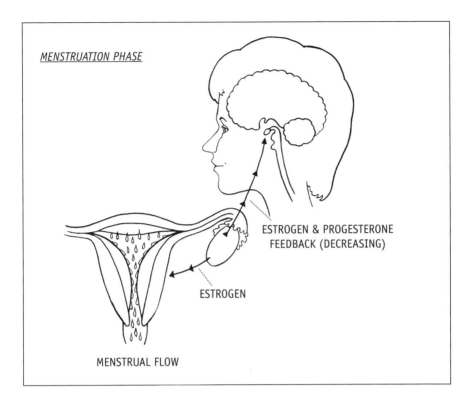

MENSTRUATION PHASE

ESTROGEN & PROGESTERONE
FEEDBACK (DECREASING)

ESTROGEN

MENSTRUAL FLOW

Menopause = "The Change of Life"

Most women go through what is called "a change of life," or menopause. It is the time when a woman stops releasing eggs and stops shedding the uterine lining through menstruation. The average age of a woman going through menopause is approximately 50. Though symptoms vary with women, one of the symptoms is commonly known as "hot flashes," meaning there is a sudden feeling of warmth that floods throughout the body. Due to the decrease in the hormonal production of estrogen and progesterone, there are often psychological and physical changes that take place in the body. For example, the lack of estrogen may bring about vaginal dryness, which then makes sexual intercourse less pleasurable. Through estrogen replacement therapy, many of these symptoms can be alleviated.

The Fallopian Tubes

Each woman has two fallopian tubes, one each located close to each ovary. On the end closest to the ovary there are small finger-like fringes called *fimbria* that sweep the space between the ovary and the tube in hopes of catching a mature egg as it is released from the ovary. When it is caught, the cilia (hair-like fringes) within the fallopian tube tissues propel the egg(s) to move toward the uterus. The journey takes three to four days. During this time, if sexual intercourse occurs, sperm will go searching for the egg. If the sperm and egg meet, fertilization (i.e., uniting of sperm and egg cell) ordinarily will occur. The fertilized egg then continues its journey toward the uterus where it will attach to the wall and continue to grow for nine months. The three or four days between ovulation and arrival of the ovum in the uterus means that there is a relatively short time in a woman's menstrual cycle when she can become pregnant.

Uterus

A common name for the uterus is *womb*. The uterus is the size of a woman's fist and shaped like a small pear. The oviduct canals enter at the very top of the uterine cavity. The lower, narrowed part of the uterus is called the *cervix*. Part of the cervix is inside the vagina. At one point, the cervix is extremely narrow, approximately the size of a toothpick, and yet expandable enough for a full-term baby to pass through it. The uterus contains muscles that are firm but expandable. During the birth of a baby, the muscles play an important role in the delivery by contracting and pushing the baby out into the cervical and vaginal canals.

Hysterectomy

A hysterectomy is a surgical removal of the uterus and sometimes the fallopian tubes and ovaries. The reasons for the surgery vary, from that of cancerous to fibroid growth to heavy bleeding. A hysterectomy does not incapacitate a woman's ability to have sexual intercourse.

The Sexual Anatomy of a Male—External Organs

God created males with two main external sex organs; the penis and the scrotum.

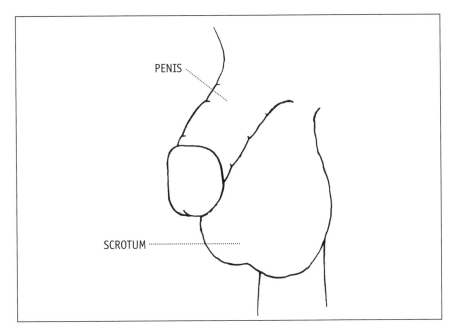

PENIS

SCROTUM

The Penis

Above the scrotal sac on a man is his reproductive and sex organ called the penis (see diagram). This organ is also used to carry urine out of the body.

At the very end of the penis is a smooth, rounded head called the *glans*. The small opening located in the center of the glans is called the *meatus*. The raised ridge surrounding the head is called the *corona*. Running down on the underside of the glans to the shaft, or the main part of the penis, is a thin band of skin called the *frenulum*.

When one is born, a skin called the foreskin covers the glans. This foreskin is often removed shortly after birth in a procedure called *circumcision*. Not all men are circumcised. In the Old Testament, circumcision symbolized the covenant between God and His people. Circumcision was, in fact, commanded by God. Those who were not circumcised were to be "cut off from His people" (Genesis 17:10–14).

With Christ's coming, circumcision is no longer required as a religious rite. Christians are said to be circumcised in Christ through Baptism:

In Him you were also circumcised, in the putting off of the sinful nature, not with a circumcision done by the hands of men but with the circumcision done by Christ, having been buried with Him in baptism and raised with Him through your faith in the power of God, who raised Him from the dead. (Colossians 2:11–12)

Far different from physical circumcision where a part of the flesh was cut off as symbolic of the covenant relationship with God, the Christian celebrates the fact that through Baptism the entire "body of flesh" is "put off."

The "putting off" is positional truth, that is, truth which obtains as a result of the believer's being placed in Christ by the Spirit's baptizing work. Because the sin nature was judged by Christ in His death, so the believer by virtue of his organic union and identification with His Lord shares that "putting off" which Christ accomplished, just as he shares Christ's fulness and is declared "to be complete in Him" (Col. 2:10).[2]

Though circumcision may still be done for religious reasons, the main argument for circumcision is hygienic. Proponents maintain that uncircumcised boys may not always want to go through the trouble of pulling back their foreskin to wash the glans.

Some fathers insist on their boys being circumcised so that they will look like them. Other arguments for circumcision: It slows down orgasm and may contribute to preventing cancer of the cervix or penis. In recent years, different anti-circumcision groups have been lobbying against circumcision, claiming that it is a needless disfigurement of the body and that it can lead to long-lasting psychological consequences.

Parents faced with the choice of circumcising their male offspring or not, will want to confer with their physician as they arrive at a decision. In any case, there are no overwhelming research data that clearly support for or anti-circumcision positions. Christians will hear the word of Scripture: "In Christ Jesus neither circumcision nor uncircumcision has any value. The only thing that counts is faith expressing itself through love" (Galatians 5:6).

The longer part of the penis, shaped like a tube, is called the *shaft*. It contains very sensitive tissues and can greatly expand when stimulated. Inside the penis is a canal called the urethra. It starts at the meatus and goes all the way back to the urinary bladder and the sperm-carrying ducts.

The size of nonerect penises varies greatly. Studies have also varied in what they claim is the size of the average nonerect male penis. Most of them say a flaccid penis is between 3.1 to 3.7 inches in length and 3.7 to 3.9 inches in circumference. Most penises even out in length and circumference at the time of erection. Shorter penises gain percentage-wise more in size than those that are longer. The average erect penis is somewhere between 5 and 7 inches long and about 4.6–4.9 inches in circumference.

Many men are overly concerned about the size of their penises. Yet there is little evidence that supports the thinking that bigger is better, except perhaps in the minds of the owners. Though some partners may prefer larger penises, one's ability to sexually satisfy another person is not in the size of one's genitals but rather in one's ability to communicate with what one has been given.

Unfortunately, man's obsession with the size of his penis has produced a market of "penis enlargement" techniques, including some that are nothing more than medical quackery. Many of them use some form of suction device. The penis is inserted into a tube while air is removed from the tube, which in most cases does nothing more than create an erection for the male, enlarging the penis only for the time it is erect.

Many larger cities have groups of physicians who specialize in the enlargement of the penis through surgery. One procedure includes inserting fat cells into the penile shaft to make the penis thicker in circumference. The techniques used have not always proven to be successful, and in fact some have actually diminished the patient's ability to maintain an erection.

When the psalmist said we are "fearfully and wonderfully made" (Psalm 139:14), this would have to include the ability God placed in a man and a woman to have sexual intercourse. Everything from the way the vagina tightens up in the front and expands out in the back during arousal, to the erection of the man's penis, is God's way of making sexual intercourse possible. He created in the male penis wonderful, small, spongy caverns so that blood could rush in to make the penis grow in length and circumference. When the penis fills with blood and gets hard, it is called an erection. Contrary to what some people believe, the ability to have an erection doesn't start in the penis. It begins in the cerebral cortex of the brain, which in turn sends messages through the nerves of the spinal cord to the penis, which stimulates or inhibits stiffness.

After ejaculation occurs, the penis returns to its normal size. The muscles that relaxed and opened during sexual excitement, allowing blood to flow into the empty caverns, now close off and no longer allow blood to flood in. (Sometimes, due to a number of circumstances, a male may lose his erection even in the midst of making love.)

Scrotum

Directly under the penis is a sac called the *scrotum* (see diagram). The scrotum contains some of the important internal reproductive organs. At puberty the scrotum begins to get darker in color. The testes, housed in the scrotum, only produce sperm when they are at a temperature lower than the temperature of the rest of the body. During puberty the scrotum begins to grow larger, which in turn allows the testes to hang lower and farther away from the body, thereby allowing sperm to be produced. On cold days, the scrotum will pull closer to the body to share its heat and prevent too *cold* a temperature for sperm production and maintenance. All of this is another sharp reminder of God's wisdom in the way He designed the male body!

The Inside Reproductive Organs of a Man

The male reproductive organs are as follows (see diagram):

1. Testes

2. Epididymis

3. Vas Deferens

4. Seminal Vesicles

5. Prostate

6. Cowper's Glands

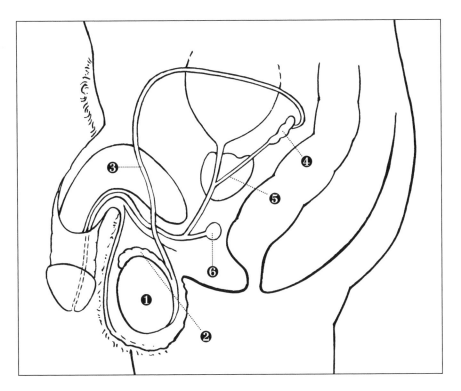

Testes

The testes are two egg-shaped organs housed in the scrotum. In each testicle there are approximately 750 feet of tiny tubes tightly coiled together. It is within these tubes that the male sperm is produced, along with some of the seminal fluid that carries the sperm through various ducts and out through the penis.

Between these tubules are cells that produce the hormone called *testosterone*. Testosterone stimulates the production of sperm. Because sperm can only be produced when the testes are at a temperature lower than the body's temperature, elastic-like cords suspend the testicles up or down to help secure the correct temperature for sperm production.

What many people fail to realize is that sperm are produced in unbelievable amounts every day of a man's life. Most men produce about 50 to 100 million a day. The typical ejaculation can contain up to 600 million sperm. When these sperm are released they all race to find one thing—the female egg. They are designed to fertilize the egg and will live for as long as three to five days inside a woman's body for that to happen.

Get Ready, Set, Go!

"As though at the starting gate of a marathon, 500 million sperm set off toward an elusive finishing line: an ovum concealed in the fallopian tube. Of this teeming crowd, only one can enter the ovum. For odds of 500 million to 1, a life-giving prize."[3]

Epididymis

Directly on top of the testis (see diagram) is another network of thread-like tubules called the *epididymis*. In these tubules sperm mature and prepare to leave the body. The release of the mature sperm is called ejaculation or emission.

In orgasm, all the muscles that tightened during sexual arousal relax, causing pleasurable sensations to flow through the body. It is uncontrollable. Orgasm and ejaculation often occur together, but not always. A boy or man can ejaculate without having an orgasm.

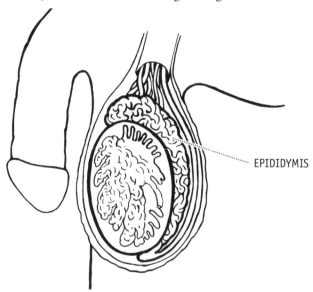

EPIDIDYMIS

Vas Deferens

The vas deferens is the long slender tube that carries sperm from the epididymis into the body cavity and to the seminal vesicles. (One tube runs from each epididymis to its corresponding seminal vesicle.)

The tubes not only serve as a road for the sperm but actually help the sperm on their journey by producing a secretion that makes them more motile.

Seminal Vesicles

At the end of each vas deferens are glands called the seminal vesicles. These produce additional seminal fluid. As the sperm pass through, this fluid mixes with them, making them even more motile.

Prostate

As the sperm continue their journey, they enter the prostate, a gland located beneath the urinary bladder. It is approximately the size of a walnut, and, doughnut shaped, encircles the urethra. (Swelling of the prostrate that often occurs as men age can cause difficulty in urinating because the swollen prostrate constricts the urethra.) The prostrate supplies yet more seminal fluid.

Prostate Problems

Prostate enlargement is common as men age. This enlargement is known as benign prostatic hypertrophy (BPH). For some men it may be the cause for frequent urination along with a sensation to urinate even after one has finished.

The prostate is susceptible to cancer, especially in older men. For this reason, every man over 50 years of age should have annual prostate examinations. In circumstances where there is a strong familial history of prostate cancer, annual examinations could be considered at age 40, but recommendations presently place them at 45. Prostate examinations usually involve two procedures: (1) a blood test called the PSA test (prostate-specific antigen), and (2) a physical examination where the physician places his finger into the rectum and feels the prostate.

Cowper's Glands

Below the prostate gland are two glands called the Cowper's glands. These glands are attached to the urethra and produce a lubricant known as pre-ejaculation fluid. This fluid coats the lining of and neutralizes acids in the urethra, making it a safer environment for the sperm. Pre-ejaculation fluid can also help lubricate the penis and vagina during intercourse.

Misconceptions over What Women Like about Men

A survey asked men which parts of a male's body were most exciting to women. The women were asked the same question.

	Men said	Women said
tallness	13%	5%
hair (texture)	4%	5%
eyes	4%	11%
neck	2%	3%
muscular neck/shoulders	21%	1%
muscular arms	18%	0%
slimness	7%	15%
flat stomach	9%	13%
buttocks	4%	39%
large penis	15%	2%
long legs	3%	6%[4]

Praising God for our Bodies

The use of slang words to describe body parts, especially our sexual and reproductive parts, says a myriad of things. By using these words we might be covering up our embarrassment over knowing so little about the human body. Using slang words to describe the different parts of the body instead of using the actual names can also convey a negative picture to our children about the human body. This is the last thing God our Father wants, especially since the body and soul are so important to Him that He was willing to send His own Son in a truly human body.

Because that Son is also now the God-*man*, He is able "to sympathize with our weaknesses" and was "tempted in every way, just as we are—yet *was without sin*" (Hebrews 4:15). As a true human, He lived without sin—for us; and also died—for us; that our bodies might be raised and glorified on the Last Day. Wow! What a reason to glorify God, *also in our bodies!* (See 1 Corinthians 6:20.)

Yes, Christians, of all people, can talk openly and respectfully of the human body, because it is, according to God, a "temple of the Holy Spirit" (1 Corinthians 6:19). And if there is one thing we can learn from the Song of Songs in the Old Testament, it is that the human body can also be appreciated as a source of great pleasure:

> Your graceful legs are like jewels,
>> the work of a craftsman's hands.
> Your navel is a rounded goblet
>> that never lacks blended wine.
> Your waist is a mound of wheat
>> encircled by lilies.
> Your breasts are like two fawns,
>> twins of a gazelle.
>> *(Songs of Songs 7:1–3)*

Ways of "Making Love"

CHAPTER 4

His left arm is under my head, and his right arm embraces me. (Song of Songs 2:6)

No one can accuse God of being boring. Look around at His creation, especially mankind. He colored His people different colors. He intricately made them different shapes and sizes. He gave them different personalities. He even created them differently as far as the size of their sexual organs. Some women He has endowed with large breasts; others with small ones. Some men He has given large penises; others small ones. Some people He covered with hair, still others are smooth.

God also created people differently as far as their likes and dislikes. Some like the taste of liver and onions, others wouldn't eat it if their life depended on it. Some like country music, others think it's too syrupy and tawdry. Some like the smell of Estée Lauder perfume, others get sick from it. Just as there is infinite variety in the foods we like, the music we listen to, and the perfume we prefer, so there is infinite variety in the way lovers communicate sexually.

There are many acceptable ways of making love within the context of marriage. What may kill more marriages than anything is simple and plain boredom. Sexual love loses its whimsical fantasy when it becomes mere ritual each week; when it is done at the same time, the same place, using the same technique. Creative lovers forget decorum; they abandon protocol, and romp and play as freely as a child who recently discovered how to ride a bicycle without training wheels. A husband and wife team that works on creativity in the bedroom will never have to worry about being bored.

> "A good sex life isn't something that
> you're born with, any more than you're
> born with the ability to cook, or crochet,
> or take shorthand."[1]

Some Forms of Intercourse

The Greeks had a variety of words to describe love. These words included *phileo* [fil-EA-o] (a friendship love where there is a sharing of thoughts and feelings), *agape* [a-GAHP-ay] (a love that is totally unselfish and has the capacity to give and keep on giving without expecting a return), *storge* [STOR-gay] (a natural affection for another person that expresses security and acceptance), and *eros* (love that is erotic, romantic, and passionate). All four of these together describe an ideal romantic love—a love that includes and indeed can find its deepest expression in the act of sexual intercourse.

The Bible identifies the marriage bond with the act of sexual intercourse as being or becoming "one flesh." To be one flesh denotes an intimate communion, as if the two were but one body or one person. Jesus said, "At the beginning the Creator 'made them male and female,' and said, 'For this reason a man will leave his father and mother and be united to his wife, and the two will become one flesh' " (Matthew 19:4–5). That's why sexual intercourse outside the bond of marriage is a gross distortion of the God-designed marriage union. Writing to the Christians at Corinth, Paul reminds them, "Do you not know that your bodies are members of Christ Himself? Shall I then take the members of Christ and unite them with a prostitute? Never! Do you not know that he who unites himself with a prostitute is one with her in body? For it is said, 'The two will become one flesh' " (1 Corinthians 6:15–16).

Sexual intercourse, thus, is of vital importance in maintaining the health of a marriage:

> *But since there is so much immorality, each man should have his own wife, and each woman her own husband. The husband should fulfill his marital duty to his wife, and likewise the wife to her husband. The*

wife's body does not belong to her alone but also to her husband. In the same way, the husband's body does not belong to him alone but also to his wife. Do not deprive each other except by mutual consent and for a time, so that you may devote yourselves to prayer. Then come together again so that Satan will not tempt you because of your lack of self-control. (1 Corinthians 7:2–5)

Because of how humans were created, husband and wife are capable of experiencing and enjoying the gift of sexual intercourse in a variety of ways.

Male-on-Top Position

The male-on-top position is also known as the "missionary position." This name was given it years ago when early missionaries had gone to the Polynesian Islands to convert the natives. When the Polynesians heard that the missionaries had sex most of the time in only one position—a face-to-face position with the man on top—they were amused because they had a variety of ways of making love, including squatting. (The squatting position is also known as the "oceanic position." The woman lies down and spreads her legs, as the man squats over her and thrusts his penis into her vagina.)

In the male-on-top position, the wife lies on her back, her legs outstretched and separated. The man lies on top of her, supporting the weight of his body by resting on his arms or elbows. If he positions himself correctly, he is able to stimulate her clitoris by rubbing his pubic bone against it as he thrusts with his penis. During the act of intercourse, the woman may wrap her legs around his body, further enhancing their sense of oneness. As the man inserts his penis inside her vagina, his position of being on top of her gives him the advantage of thrusting deeper and with greater impact than many other positions.

Female-on-Top Position

In this position, the man lies on his back. As his wife sits on him, she tilts forward and moves her vagina onto his penis. In this position, the woman has control over the amount of thrusting that the man is able to do, and can be more active in her own thrusting. In this way she can better time his orgasm as well as her own. This position gives the man an opportunity to use his hands, either caressing her breasts or stimulating her clitoris. Men are also able to hold off longer in ejaculating in this female-superior position.

Side-by-Side Position (or Lateral Position)

In this position, neither partner places his or her weight on the other. The partners lie next to each other. This position requires that the woman spread her legs by placing one leg between her husband's legs and the other one over the lower part of his body as he inserts his penis into her vagina. Upon insertion, both partners are able to use at least one of their hands for touching the other. The advantage is that no one partner has to bear the weight of his or her spouse.

Male-Behind Position

Especially when the wife is pregnant, the male-behind position may provide advantages. The woman kneels on all fours, or lies on her stomach. The man straddles his wife, and enters her vagina from behind. The advantage of this position during pregnancy is obvious. Whenever this position is used, it gives the man free access to caress and fondle almost any part of his wife's body as intercourse takes place.

The positions just described are the primary ones used by most couples who seek orgasm through the penis being inserted in the vagina. One can be assured, there are many variations on the same theme. A couple somewhat athletic and adventuresome may find intercourse most pleasurable through something called a "standing-up position." The man picks up the woman, and, as she wraps her legs around his body, he thrusts his penis into her vagina. Still another couple might find the "oceanic position," or the "squatting position," referred to earlier, as the most pleasurable. The position two people choose to use is not what's important; the lovemaking itself is.

"There is no norm in sex. Norm is the name of a guy who lives in Brooklyn."[2]

Oral Sex

Oral sex is the stimulation of another person's genitalia with the mouth. It is called *fellatio* when it involves licking or sucking the penis. It is called *cunnilingus* when it involves licking or sucking the woman's vulva area, especially her clitoris. Statistics show that over 75 percent of married couples engage in oral sex. Though many members of both sexes seem to find oral sex pleasurable, studies indicate that men find it especially stimulating. Some men will verbally pressure their unwilling wives into performing fellatio on them. It must always be remembered that for any sexual act to be right, it must be right in God's eyes first, and it must also be acceptable and right in the eyes of both partners. One must always consider "the good of others" as St. Paul says in 1 Corinthians 10:24.

Oral sex can be so important to a man or woman that if it is withheld in the marriage relationship, it can literally tempt a person into another relationship. An older man, married for 40 years, came to my office and confessed that he had been unfaithful to his wife. His rationalization was, "I'm embarrassed to tell you this, but you need to know why I'm having the affair. For years I've wanted someone to perform oral sex on me. I've been married for 40 years and never in those 40 years has my wife as much as touched my penis with her mouth. My new girlfriend loves oral sex, in fact she ..."

For this man, the desire for oral sex literally mastered him and led him into an adulterous affair. When I asked him if he had ever discussed the desire he had with his wife he said, "No, because I know what she would have said."

The health of any couple depends on good communication, talking to one another about every aspect of sexuality, including oral sex.

Some suggest that reference to oral sex is made when the writer of the Song of Songs invites his lover to "come into his garden and taste its choice fruits" (Song of Songs 4:16). At the same time, the lover speaks of having gathered "myrrh with ... spice ... honeycomb and ... honey ... wine and ... milk" (Song of Songs 5:1). The lover claims the garden as his own. He speaks of gathering the fruits of the garden and eating and drinking these fruits.

"I cannot help asking whether we do not, in that very heat of extreme gratification when the generative fluid is ejected, feel that somewhat of our soul has gone out from us? And do we not experience a faintness and prostration along with a dimness of sight? This, then, must be the soul-producing seed, which arises from the outdrip of the soul, just as that fluid is the body-producing seed which proceeds from the drainage of the flesh.

"In a single impact of both parties, the whole human frame is shaken and foams with semen in which the damp humour of the body is joined to the hot substance of the soul."[3]

Anal Sex

Anal sex is the insertion of the penis into the partner's anus. Though the anus has nerve endings, God placed this opening into the body for quite a different reason than copulation. In God's design, the anus is there to rid the body of fecal matter stored up in the colon. When it does, despite the amount of wiping or washing that may occur, germs still remain in the passageway, making it in many respects an unsafe place for penis penetration. The anus was also not designed to endure the steady thrusting of a penis or any other object. With such thrusting, anal tissue will often break and bleed.

Frequency of Lovemaking

Somewhere one hears that the average couple has sex 2.3 times a week, and so begins to think one must be at least average or above in copulation frequency each week. Such thinking is only part of the "muchness and manyness" thinking of our day. The bottom line is, it is not the number of times one makes love with his or her spouse, or the number of times one brings his or her spouse to orgasm. What is most important is that both husband and wife have the right attitude toward lovemaking and do everything they can do to satisfy each another. What is enough or not enough in bed should be determined by the husband and wife, not by statistics. What the "average couple" does might not be sufficient for you and your spouse at all. You do not have to meet the needs of other people, simply the needs of each other.

"We do not dare to classify or compare ourselves with some who commend themselves. When they measure themselves by themselves and compare themselves with themselves, they are not wise."
(2 Corinthians 10:12)

The Making of Love through Outercourse

The expression of love to another takes on many forms. For one couple it might be to sit together in front of the television set holding each other's hands. For still another it might be to take a shower together and, simply by stroking and touching one another's bodies, bring about mutual orgasm without ever having penile penetration. Much of this type of activity used to be called "petting"; however, for a variety of reasons, this term is seldom used today. Now the term *outercourse* describes some of these alternatives to intercourse.

Using Baseball Terminology
Though few men today use baseball terminology to describe their sexual activity, years ago they did. When they talked about their date they would talk about "making it to first base" or "getting to third base." Seldom did they talk about "making a home run," because it meant having had sexual intercourse. "Making it to first base" usually included kissing in the car before one escorted his girlfriend back to her front door. "Getting to second base" may have meant parking in "lover's lane" overlooking the city lights and steaming up the car with kissing and some caressing of each other's genitals with the clothes still on. "Getting to third base" referred to much of what today is called "outercourse." It may have included undressing, stroking each other's bodies, and perhaps even mutual masturbation.

There are many types of outercourse that couples use to express their love for one another. Some of these forms include mutual masturbation without intercourse, tongue bathing, giving and receiving sensual massages, rubbing bodies together, and the use of sex toys. Though some of these forms of outercourse may not be appealing to every couple, in and by themselves there is nothing wrong with them when they are used in a marriage relationship to further accentuate and heighten the couple's sexual experience.

A vibrator can be a useful tool if used to help ready a spouse for orgasm or when sexual intercourse isn't possible. Mutual masturbation might help convey to one's partner which areas are especially sensitive to touch. Tongue bathing, where a couple uses their tongues to lick and kiss each other all over, can not only be an unforgettable sensual experience; it can also help each partner understand more about his or her own body as well as his or her partner's.

If one of the partners has been unfaithful and trust has been broken, one of the areas of the couple's life that may be the most difficult to mend is in the area of their sexual relationship. In this instance, massage, without genital intercourse, might be one way to begin to rebuild trust and intimacy. Trust comes with time and honest communication. As the partners gently massage each other's bodies, each can learn much from the other's verbal and physical responses.

Whether or not any of these forms of outercourse are sinful will depend in large part on one's thinking and mind-set, just as in intercourse itself. If while using a vibrator, one fantasizes lustfully about someone else, removing oneself from his or her partner emotionally and psychologically, the use of it then becomes wrong and a hindrance to a couple's oneness, their being "one flesh." Jesus makes it clear that fantasizing lustfully about another person is the same as committing adultery with that person (Matthew 5:28).

As Christians, we strive to bring our thoughts into obedience to Christ and His ways: "We take captive every thought to make it obedient to Christ" (2 Corinthians 10:5). However, when sex toys are used to further add stimulation and heighten the couple's sexual experience and their love for each other, most Christian marriage counselors would agree that they are perfectly acceptable ways of expressing love.

Remember, God created us with different likes and dislikes. What is important is that you discuss whatever you might want to do with your spouse before trying it. Four rules are important as you consider the suggested ways of lovemaking: (1) Don't ask or expect something of your spouse that he or she vehemently objects to doing. (2) Don't do something you don't really enjoy. (3) Find out the needs of one another through honest and loving communication. (4) Don't do anything that is contrary to God's Word, such as doing harm to each other physically or emotionally.

Adult Sexual Response

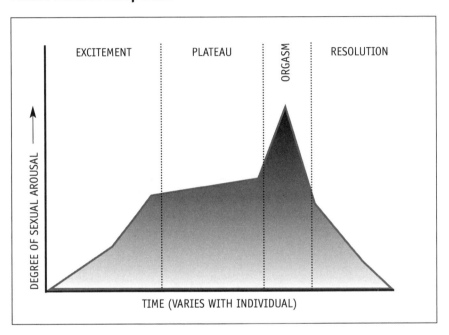

Most people go through a pattern of response when sexually stimulated. This pattern is called our sexual response cycle. There are usually five elements in this cycle: (1) desire, (2) excitement, (3) plateau, (4) orgasm, and (5) resolution. Some may not experience orgasm; nevertheless, there can still be sexual fulfillment. As we review this response cycle, we cannot help but know that something that works so well, that fits together so intricately, did not happen by pure chance. It could only happen by design, a design that God put together. We must exclaim with the psalmist: "The fool says in his heart, 'There is no God' " (Psalm 14:1).

The most sensual part of the body
is the imagination.

"How Will This Drug Affect My Sexual Functioning?"
Whenever drugs are prescribed, one of the questions that should automatically be asked is whether or not it will affect one's ability to function sexually. For example, some drugs prescribed for heart attack patients, as well as those suffering from depression, may affect a person's sexual desire. Others may affect one's ability to get and maintain an erection. Some affect a man's ability to ejaculate or a woman's ability to have an orgasm. Often, doctors can prescribe alternative medications that do not interfere with one's sexual functioning.

The Desire Phase

God gave humans five different senses—tasting, smelling, seeing, hearing, and touching. These senses can attract or distract. The way he looks at you before you go off to bed may say more than a thousand words. The perfume she dabs on before she reaches the bed may elicit desire. The way he talks to you at the breakfast table may say to you, "I can hardly wait to get home tonight." Her pat on your fanny as you're cleaning up the kitchen after dinner might be saying a myriad of things about her desire for intimacy.

Some would call this phase the prelude to lovemaking, much like the prelude to a worship service. A good prelude before worship sets the mood for all of worship. And so the prelude to lovemaking sets the mood for the celebration in the bedroom later.

Dr. Kevin Leman, in his book, *Sex Begins in the Kitchen*, reminds us that sex does not begin and end under the covers, but is something that starts "early in the morning."

> *"Sex is an all-day affair. It starts early in the morning and culminates at a later time in a very healthy and loving way, providing the groundwork has been laid for the sexual reunion ... The key element in making the sex act exciting is for a man to understand that he must be gentle, loving, and caring in all things. It's a matter of, do you love your wife, meet her needs, put her priorities first in your life? Does she come out number one in the various facets of your life? Are you genuinely concerned about her, about her day?"[4]*

The phase of desire varies with people. It can be short in duration, five or ten minutes. It can be long in duration, a few days or weeks.

The Excitement Phase

Excitement often follows a period of desire. What starts in the mind travels to the genitalia. One or more of the senses triggers a bodily reaction. Some experts claim that our bodies actually produce certain chemical substances called pheromones that play an important role in this process. The brain is also known to be stimulated by phenylethlamine (PEA), which produces elation and euphoria.

Excitement stirs a person toward outercourse and/or intercourse. During the excitement phase many things happen in each partner. (See chart on page 75.)

Response During the Excitement Phase of Lovemaking

Female Response

Increase of heart rate and blood pressure

A blushing or a reddening, called a "sex flush," of the upper part of the body (i.e., chest, neck, forehead)

Erection of the nipples and increase in the size of the breasts

Engorging or enlarging of the clitoris (up to two or three times its normal size)

Flattening and opening of the outer lips (labia majora)

Enlarging of the inner lips (labia minora)

Lubrication of the vagina

Elevation of the uterus

Male Response

Increase of heart rate and blood pressure

A blushing or reddening, called a "sex flush," of the upper part of the body (i.e., chest, neck, forehead)

Erection of the nipples

Erection of the penis

A thickening of the scrotum

A drawing up of the testes closer to the body

Is it any wonder that the Holy Scriptures declare, "God saw all that He had made, and it was very good" (Genesis 1:31)? Into His created humans, He had intricately woven muscles, nerves, and glands to prepare the body for sexual intercourse. It isn't by accident that at the time of excitement the vagina begins to secrete beads of lubrication. It is by design—His design—to enhance pleasure and help reduce friction upon the insertion of the penis. It isn't byt accident that the outer lips spread out flat. It is by design—God's design—as a way of poreparing for the entrance of the penis. It isn't by accident that ythe testes draw claser to the body so that the seminal fluid within may be warmed in order to better travel in search of an egg. It is by design—God's design. "Let everything that has breath praise the Lord. Praise the Lord" (Psalm 150:6).

The Importance of Touching

One of the most intimate forms of communication is touch. It is the source of much physical pleasure, not only for the one being touched, but also for the one who is touching. Learning the art of massage can enhance lovemaking greatly.

"Studies show that being touched can actually lower a person's blood pressure. Low blood pressure is an important part of staying healthy. But that's not all. In a recent study at UCLA, it was found that just to maintain emotional and physical health, men and women need eight to ten meaningful touches each day!"[5]

The Plateau Phase

During the plateau phase, stimulation continues. The stimulation may include everything from caressing the breasts to the thrusting of the penis into the vagina. It can include licking and kissing each other's nipples and/or the rubbing of the clitoris. By placing many erogenous zones within the body, God has provided man and woman with a myriad of opportunities to give each other sexual pleasure.

It is during the plateau phase that most men and women find it extremely difficult to stop intercourse or outercourse. During this phase pre-ejaculatory fluid seeps from the penis, further lubricating the vagina. The pre-ejaculatory fluid does contain some sperm, and so withdrawing before there is full ejaculation does not assure a couple that there will be no pregnancy. The most notable changes that occur during this time are noted on the following chart.

Response During the Plateau Phase of Lovemaking

Female Response

Heart rate and blood pressure continue to increase

Breathing intensifies

Blushing or reddening may continue to increase

The areolas, the dark area surrounding the nipples, continue to increase in size

There is further enlargement of the clitoris as it withdraws and hides under the clitoral hood, becoming extremely sensitive to direct touch and more difficult to locate

The outer lips (labia majora) continue to thicken

The inner lips (labia minora) become redder in color and continue to swell

The vagina narrows and tightens near the opening and widens near the uterus

The Bartholin's glands continue to provide lubrication of the vagina

There is full elevation of the uterus

The cervix pulls farther away from the thrusting penis

Male Response

Heart rate and blood pressure continue to increase

Breathing intensifies

Blushing or reddening may continue to increase

Pre-ejaculation fluid is produced by the Cowper's glands

Glans enlargement

Testes enlargement

Testes continue to draw closer to the body

Once again we see God's creation as being "good." The Penners note God's wonderful design:

It is as if God designed the vagina to tighten up in the front and expand or balloon out in the back for several purposes. In terms of the reproductive purpose of intercourse, this change keeps the seminal fluid containing the sperm inside the vagina. There is now a small base or pool at the back of the vagina where the seminal fluid can gather, so that, as the opening to the uterus falls back into place after the sexual experience, the sperm can travel up through the cervix into the uterus.[6]

The Orgasm Phase

The orgasm phase is the fourth stage of the sexual response cycle. In this phase, all the muscles that tightened over the last two phases relax, and the man ejaculates. For the man, orgasm occurs because of contractions that take place in the prostate and seminal vesicles. As these contract, they move (ejaculate) the semen out of the penis. This release is called "having an orgasm."

The majority of women also experience orgasm at this time. Though there is a wide range of thinking on what orgasm actually is for a woman, the research of Masters and Johnson found that for most women, orgasm consists of contractions in the outer third of the vagina as well as in the uterus. Some men base their own sexual prowess on their ability to bring their wives to orgasm, and yet studies show that sexual satisfaction for many women does not depend on orgasm at all.

What some couples fail to realize is that there are distinct differences in the way men and women experience orgasm. Men usually have one orgasm during this cycle of sexual response. Women can have numerous ones. Men are unable to interrupt or stop ejaculation from occurring once it's started. Women are capable of stopping their orgasms if there is some interruption, such as a child suddenly entering the bedroom. For men, though orgasm is all-encompassing—physically, emotionally, and spiritually—it is even more so for women. It is much more difficult for her to simply turn over and not continue radiating the warmth and satisfaction that she has just experienced.

The orgasm phase is the shortest of all phases. On average it lasts a minute or less. The responses during this phase in each partner are noted on the following chart.

Response During the Orgasm Phase of Lovemaking

Female Response

Heart rate reaches its highest level

Breathing intensifies to its highest level

Blushing or reddening may spread over other parts of the body

There are involuntary muscular movements

Muscles within the vagina, uterus, anus, and those surrounding the pelvic area may contract

Male Response

Heart rate reaches its highest level

Breathing intensifies to its highest level

Blushing or reddening may spread over other parts of the body

There are involuntary muscular movements

Ejaculation

Muscles within the urethra, anus, and those surrounding the pelvic area may contract

---

At the time of orgasm, the brain releases a chemical called endorphin. This chemical in turn produces a feeling of relaxation, calmness, and tranquillity within the lovers. In considering that God, in His infinite wisdom, knew how to provide such pleasure here on earth through sexual intercourse—the ecstasy of orgasm—it is no wonder that when we think of heaven and what He has prepared for us there that we must exclaim "No eye has seen, no ear has heard, no mind has conceived what God has prepared for those who love Him" (1 Corinthians 2:9).

The Resolution Phase

The last phase of the sexual response cycle is known as the "resolution phase," or "relaxation phase." The man is no longer aroused, and loses his erection. There is a period of time (the refractory period) when he is unable to get another erection. The time of the refractory period depends a great deal on the age of the man. Younger men are usually able to produce another erection much sooner than many older men.

The resolution phase is a time when the body returns to the way it was before becoming excited and aroused, before orgasm took place.

Response During the Resolution Phase of Lovemaking

<u>Female Response</u>

Heart rate levels off to normal

The entire body perspires

The breasts and the outer and inner lips (labia majora and labia minora) return to normal size

The clitoris comes out from the clitoral hood and returns to its normal size

The cervix continues to stay open so that semen might travel in search for a possible egg

Approximately a half hour after orgasm the uterus moves back to the upper part of the vagina

<u>Male Response</u>

Heart rate levels off to normal

The entire body perspires

The nipples, penis, and scrotum return to normal size

The testes descend away from the body to their normal position

---

Earlier we talked about the importance of the prelude at the beginning of a worship service. It prepares the worshipers for celebration. Equally important is the postlude. It is to enhance what has already taken place in worship. It is done in the same spirit as the rest of the service. So the resolution phase of making love is like the postlude for the celebration that just took place in the bedroom. Two people have celebrated their oneness in the most intimate way possible, through sexual intercourse or outercourse. The postlude, the epilog of the experience, involves caressing and holding each other, maybe talking to one another, maybe doing nothing at all but falling asleep in each other's arms. The postlude of lovemaking involves caring about how the other person is feeling as much as you care about yourself.

Often men find this part of lovemaking to be the most difficult. If so, it is wise to remember the words of St. Paul: "Husbands, love your wives, just as Christ loved the church and gave Himself up for her to make her holy" (Ephesians 5:25–26). Think about God's tenderness and kindness toward us. God is never too tired to tenderly hold us, to talk to us, to affirm who we are in and through Jesus Christ. Our love for one another is to be expressed in the same way. "Love each other as I have loved you," Jesus said (John 15:12). On our own we can't love others as He has loved us, but we can with His help, even when we're tired, even when we feel like turning over and just falling asleep.

"Women need a reason for sex. Men need a place." (from the movie *City Slickers*, 1991)

 "A couple in marriage is called to worship God as much by their trothful, erotic sex as by their prayers for each other. All that God has given to us can enrich our well-being and enjoyment."[7]

CHAPTER 5

Sex and the Single Person

Now to the unmarried and the widows I say: It is good for them to stay unmarried, as I am. But if they cannot control themselves, they should marry, for it is better to marry than to burn with passion. (1 Corinthians 7:8–9)

The segments of the population who seem to be most pressured sexually are the young and the unmarried. In a society that is still predominantly coupled, a single adult who is not married is often looked at suspiciously. It may not be said out loud, but there is a subtle implication that there must be something wrong with the person. The innuendoes, the questions, the pressure sometimes lead singles to prove they're normal, at least sexually. They simply move in with a member of the opposite sex. That may be one reason that the majority of people who marry today have lived together before they get married.

Surveys tell us that young people are having sex at an earlier and earlier age, often because they feel pressured into it by their peers. Because of this, it is not uncommon to hear of 13- year-old girls becoming pregnant.

The patterns are crystal clear. About half the teenagers of various racial and ethnic groups in the nation have begun having intercourse with a partner in the age range of fifteen to eighteen, and at least four out of five have had intercourse by the time their teenage years are over. Since the average age of marriage is now in the mid-twenties, few Americans wait until they marry to have sex.[1]

When men were asked why they had sexual intercourse before marriage, most of them said they "simply wanted to." In contrast to men, many of the women said they had sexual intercourse before marriage because they "were in love."[2] Because of this, single men and women often come together with different sexual agendas. The end result is confusion and disappointment.

Added to the large number of men and women who have never married are those who have divorced and are single once again. Statistics tell us that 50–55 percent of all couples who get married will divorce. The question seldom asked, but one that needs to be answered, is "How do people who have known the enjoyment of sexual oneness suddenly handle celibacy?" Or is celibacy, once you've had sex, simply out of the question?

Celibacy

Celibacy is when one does not have partner sex. This is often by choice but not always. Those who have been hurt physically in an accident or because of illness may not be celibate by choice. One of the best known celebrities who lived a life of celibacy was Jesus.

A *eunuch* is someone who is castrated—his testes are removed. This was often done to those who served as attendants in Oriental courts and under the Roman emperors. For example, Philip met an Ethiopian eunuch on the desert road to Gaza. He was "an important official in charge of all the treasury of Candace, queen of the Ethiopians" (Acts 8:27).

What about those who are single again by death of a spouse? Do they suddenly become asexual because they've lost a spouse? Even if they're older? Of course not! Though one's sexual functioning may decline with age, one's desire for intimacy through sexual union does not disappear!

"Mum's the word. The clergy, once loquacious on the topic of premarital 'sin,' are equally subdued. 'Have you ever heard a sermon on living together?' asked religious columnist Michael McManus in his 1995 book, *Marriage Savers*. Condemnation of adult premarital sex has virtually vanished from religious preaching, even in the homilies of Catholic priests. 'In the pulpits there has been a backing away from moralizing about sex before marriage,' says Bishop James McHugh, the bishop of Camden, N.J.

"Why such reticence? The answer may seem obvious. Americans, at least tacitly, have all but given up on the notion that the appropriate premarital state is one of chastity. The Bible may have warned that like the denizens of Sodom and Gomorrah, those who give 'themselves over to fornication' will suffer 'the vengeance of eternal fire.' Yet for most Americans, adult premarital sex has become the 'sin' they not only wink at but quietly endorse. On television, adult virgins are as rare as caribou in Manhattan. Several studies have found that prime-time network shows implicitly condone premarital sex, and air as many as eight depictions of it for every one of sex between married couples."[3]

But Then There's God to Deal With!

Whether we care to believe it or not, the truth of the matter is that the majority of adults today—married and single—are having sex. The proof of it can be seen in the fact that one out of three children that are born today are born out of wedlock, and not only to unwed teenage mothers and fathers, but also to unwed older mothers and fathers.

If the majority of unmarried adults are having sex, what kind of sex is it? Simply put, it is uncommitted sex. This is always true, no matter what the participants claim. Sex outside of marriage is uncommitted sex, period. It can be nothing else. You can dress it up, clean it up, shine it up, and give it a nice-sounding name, but you cannot change its very nature.[4]

The promiscuity and acceptance of sex before and outside of marriage makes the church's message—that of abstinence before marriage—seem simply out-of-date and unrealistic! Many Christian moms don't even think twice about providing their teenagers with condoms and birth control pills, because "everyone is doing it, and so it's better, at least, to play it safe." Those who have been married, and are now divorced, might even laugh at a church that suggests that they abstain from sex, especially since they are so "used to having it whenever they wanted to." However, all the rationalizations and arguments in the world do not minimize God's Word and the truthfulness of it. Nor does it prove that it's impossible to keep within God's boundaries if one so chooses.

"Don't die of ignorance. Every time you sleep with a boy you sleep with all his old girlfriends."[5]

Fewer Virgins

The argument given by some single people that "it's hard to find a virgin today!" might be truer than we want to believe. "In the 1960s, 25 percent of young men and 45 percent of young women were virgins at age 19. By the 1980s, fewer than 20 percent of males and females were."[6]

God is clear. "Making love," intercourse, and outercourse are reserved for marriage! So how does one accomplish such a feat if one is single? Be assured, God does not hold out standards for us that are impossible to keep. He doesn't taunt His people by holding out something to them that is never meant to be within reach.

The truth of the matter is, some can't help but succumb to the temptations of the world around them, because they don't have the power to resist temptation. They are non-Christians. Christians have the power, by the Spirit of God indwelling in them, to choose right from wrong, not to be sexually promiscuous, to live a life of sexual abstinence. If one doesn't believe this, one needs to review carefully the Word of God:

Through these He has given us His very great and precious promises, so that through them you may participate in the divine nature. (2 Peter 1:4)

I can do everything through Him who gives me strength. (Philippians 4:13)

And God is faithful; He will not let you be tempted beyond what you can bear. But when you are tempted, He will also provide a way out so that you can stand up under it. (1 Corinthians 10:13)

One can choose not to be obedient, but then it is not because one can't be but because one won't be obedient. God gives us the power to live up to the standards He places before us.

The truth of the matter is, Christians fail in upholding God's standards, despite all the power that is theirs. Like St. Paul, we say, "For what I want to do I do not do, but what I hate I do. ... What a wretched man I am! Who will rescue me from this body of death? Thanks be to God—through Jesus Christ our Lord!" (Romans 7:15, 24). His forgiveness does not mean we can go out and sin all the more, but instead it means we will have the desire and the freedom to live even more within the boundaries He sets for us because we know He loves us. "Shall we go on sinning so that grace may increase? By no means! We died to sin; how can we live in it any longer?" (Romans 6:1–2).

Suggestions for Sexual Singles

1. Search God's Word for His truths on marriage, singleness, and sex.
2. Admit your inability to say no, and ask God to help you with your sexual urges, your temptations, your desire to "go to bed with someone you care about deeply."
3. Talk to the person you date about your morals and standards before they are challenged.
4. Make plans for situations you may have to confront someday, such as when the person you're dating says to you, "If you love me, you'll have sex with me" or "Let's do it; I have protection."
5. Keep examining your outercourse, the things you're doing to show affection (other than having sexual intercourse), such as kissing and touching each other.
6. Even if you have failed to hold up to God's standards or your own, don't give up! Confess your sin. Receive the forgiveness Christ won for you. Recommit yourself to celibacy.
7. Assure the person you're dating that in rejecting sex, you're not rejecting him or her.
8. Ask fellow Christians to help keep you accountable to God's standards.

A Definition of "Safe Sex!"

Masturbation

Singles often control their sexual urges by masturbating. Masturbation is the deliberate stimulation of the sex organs to produce sexual sensations and usually orgasm. It is also called "autoeroticism" (*auto* meaning "self" and *eroticism* meaning "sexual stimulation"). Though few people talk about it, masturbation is common among most adults. A study done by Michael, Gagnon, Laumann, and Kolata found that "among Americans aged eighteen to fifty-nine, about 60 percent of the men and 40 percent of the women said they masturbated in the past year. About one man in four and one woman in ten reported that they masturbate at least once a week."[7]

There are many reasons why any discussion of masturbation is taboo. Among Christians, masturbation has often been thought to be sinful and condemned by God. Some people have condemned it on the basis of Genesis 38:4–10 where Onan "spilled his semen on the ground"

(v. 9). God struck Onan dead, but not for the reasons some Christians say—for spilling semen on the ground—but instead for disobeying God's command to help bear a child for his deceased brother. Because some Christians have misinterpreted this scriptural passage, they call masturbation "onanism."

Judaism and Christianity are certainly not the only religions to blame for a skewed view on masturbation. In the eighteenth century, there was a very active campaign against masturbation. In a book entitled *Onanism: A Treatise on the Disorders of Masturbation*, a Swiss doctor suggested that masturbation created an imbalance in a person's body fluid, causing diseases such as tuberculosis. This immediately labeled those who suffered from this disease and others as excessive masturbators. Masturbation, he contended, could also cause grave emotional problems.

Throughout the years, many have joined in the parade of warning against the dangers of masturbation. They often gave more than warnings. Some would give advice on how to control masturbatory urges. Leading entrepreneurs such as J. H. Kellogg and Sylvester Graham suggested that the eating of their products—corn flakes and graham crackers—would prevent masturbation. Kellogg wrote extensively about certain signs and symptoms of children who were engaged in masturbation. These signs included nail biting and acne.

Fallacies about Masturbation

Though some warnings must be given about masturbation, other fallacies must be dispelled. Some of these fallacies are as follows:

1. *The majority of people who masturbate are adolescents, single people, and those who have no sexual outlet with another partner.* Studies show that those who masturbate the most are those who are sexually active with another person.[8] The highest rates of masturbation seem to be among those who are 25 to 50 years of age.

2. *Masturbation can cause one to get physically and mentally ill.* Though most people today are well aware that masturbation does not cause one to go blind or grow hair on one's palms, there are still some mistaken ideas about what it might do. For example, some athletic

coaches have been known to warn their players to avoid masturbation the night before playing an important game. Studies have shown that masturbation does not hinder one's ability to perform on the athletic field the next day.

3. *Masturbation can be as sexually satisfying as sexual intercourse.* Ultimate sexual satisfaction, as God planned it, is in the act of two people coming together physically, emotionally, and spiritually. Though masturbation may provide an avenue for sexual release and pleasure, it cannot replace what God calls "becoming one flesh."

4. *Masturbation signals that one may be homosexual or may lead one to a same-gender orientation.* The reasoning behind this is that those who are interested in their own sexual organs will be attracted to their own gender. No study has shown that masturbation leads people to change their gender orientation.

Question: "The other night I wanted to tell my son something. I opened his bedroom door without knocking and found him masturbating. … What should have I said to him?"

Answer: First of all, remember that your son isn't doing anything that most teenagers aren't doing. Over 90 percent of all teenage boys masturbate. Second, whatever you say, say it in love. Don't overreact. If you are too harsh and judgmental, you might indirectly be telling him that there's something wrong or sinful with his private parts or that he is a "pervert." As you lovingly talk to your child, express your hope that he won't become overly obsessed with masturbation, warn him that he should not stimulate his private parts in public, and talk with him about the spiritual dangers of lustful fantasizing.

Truths about Masturbation

Though there are fallacies surrounding the act of masturbation, there are also some truths that need to be remembered:

1. Masturbation is wrong when a person gets "so wrapped up in the experience of masturbation that normal social relationships may be

ignored or the God-given inclination toward marriage and inter-course [is] derailed."[9]

2. Masturbation is wrong when it interferes with a normal sexual relationship with one's spouse. In counseling, Georgette confided that she masturbated often to reach orgasm. Though she and her husband engaged in sexual activity regularly, she said she seldom had an orgasm, even though at times she pretended she did. When asked if she had ever talked to her husband about this, she said she couldn't because of embarrassment, as well as the possibility of damaging her husband's ego. She just knew that if she mentioned anything to him, it would "make him feel less manly" that he was not able to bring her to orgasm.

   Georgette's mistake is in not talking to her husband about this concern. In one sense, she is accepting a second-rate sexual experience instead of enjoying the pleasures encompassed by being "one flesh."

3. Masturbation is wrong when it is so consuming that it takes time away from family or work. Any behavior can become addictive and cause one to lose perspective. The apostle Paul warns us against being in bondage to anything: " 'Everything is permissible for me'—but not everything is beneficial. 'Everything is permissible for me'—but I will not be mastered by anything" (1 Corinthians 6:12).

4. Masturbation is wrong when it is motivated by images of people other than one's spouse. Though studies have shown that not all people who masturbate do so with images fabricated in their own mind or from pornographic material, many people do masturbate with images of people other than their spouse. God's Word makes it clear that even this is a form of adultery and is wrong: "But I tell you that anyone who looks at a woman lustfully has already committed adultery with her in his heart" (Matthew 5:28).

5. Masturbation can be a means of learning about one's own body, sexual feelings, and responsiveness. The need to explore and understand one's body and its functions can be seen early on when chil-

dren are very young. Though young children cannot have an orgasm, they do learn they can receive pleasure by touching themselves "down there." As men and women explore their bodies, they can learn not only what an orgasm feels like but how to better achieve one when making love with their spouse.

Sexual Fantasizing

Most people—men and women—fantasize. One study suggested that men have thoughts about sex every 29 seconds. Fantasies may include such things as having sex with two women at the same time or watching another couple have sex.

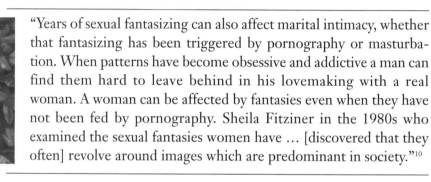

"Years of sexual fantasizing can also affect marital intimacy, whether that fantasizing has been triggered by pornography or masturbation. When patterns have become obsessive and addictive a man can find them hard to leave behind in his lovemaking with a real woman. A woman can be affected by fantasies even when they have not been fed by pornography. Sheila Fitziner in the 1980s who examined the sexual fantasies women have … [discovered that they often] revolve around images which are predominant in society."[10]

Some distinguish between fantasy and lust. They say the difference is in whether or not one hopes the thought will be carried out in action. They describe fantasy as a thought without any intention to act; lust as the hope that it will be carried out with real people and in real places.

The reality is that fantasy can turn to lust. Scripture warns us, that as we think within ourselves, so we are (see text note of Proverbs 23:7). St. Paul reminds us that the center of our being must be subject to the Lordship of Christ: "We demolish arguments and every pretension that sets itself up against the knowledge of God, and we take captive every thought to make it obedient to Christ" (2 Corinthians 10:5).

The content of most of our sexual fantasies is often shared with no one. For a married couple, sharing fantasies actually may enhance the couple's relationship. For example, if a husband reveals to his wife that he has always secretly desired that she would come to bed wearing "sexy lingerie," she could fulfill his fantasy by doing that very thing some night.

Other fantasizing can be unhealthy and dangerous to the marriage, such as when a husband or wife suggests a threesome or mate swapping.

Fantasizing is a reality. Everyone fantasizes. But in our fantasizing, our prayer must be that it will be as God instructs us:

Finally, brothers, whatever is true, whatever is noble, whatever is right, whatever is pure, whatever is lovely, whatever is admirable— if anything is excellent or praiseworthy—think about such things. Whatever you have learned or received or heard from me, or seen in me—put it into practice. And the God of peace will be with you. (Philippians 4:8–9)

Top Five Fantasies

1. Having sex in a threesome (40%)
2. Using a video camera (28%)
3. Bondage (24%)
4. Having an orgy (22%)
5. Taking photographs (20%)[11]

Rape and Date Rape

Single people are reporting more incidences of sexual coercion and/or rape than ever before. The frequency of occurrence has been greatly influenced by the high use of alcohol and drugs among young people. With more incidences being reported, the definition of what actually constitutes a rape has been debated, especially when the person being accused is a friend or a date.

Most agree that rape is the physical forcing of someone who is unwilling to perform a sexual act. This physical force can come in the way of restraints or assault and threat. A "date rape," or as it sometimes is called, "acquaintance rape," is also the forcing of an unwilling person to perform a sexual act, but added to this is the fact that the person forcing the other person is someone the victim knows. They may even be on a date together.

Recently, something called "marital rape" has been introduced into the courts. It takes place when there isn't mutual consent between both marriage partners.

Constructive Force

"Constructive force" means that because of an unequal relationship between an instructor and trainee, a military officer of higher rank who takes advantage sexually of someone of lower rank can be charged with rape. A weapon or a threat does not have to accompany the act.

Sexual coercion can take on many forms. It can include verbal pressure and/or physical pressure. Whatever the way, rape is a violent act and is illegal. In God's eyes it is also wrong. In an age when so often the secular world disagrees with God's ways, it is interesting that both are in agreement over this issue.

"A 1993 study of women at three Midwestern universities showed that of all the women surveyed, 42 percent had been victims of some sort of sexual coercion in dating situations while at college."[12]

Making Sure "Yes" Is Yes and "No" Is No

Singles of all people must make it clear to those they date what they believe about sex before marriage. Hopefully, these beliefs and morals will be based on God's Word. The lordship of Christ is really the alpha and the omega in all sexual matters, whether it be in the sexual desire one has or in the act of lovemaking itself.

Needless to say, to follow Christ's ways instead of those advocated by culture is not always easy. For this reason, a Christian's "yes" must be clearly spoken when "yes" is meant, and "no" clearly spoken when it is meant. James reminds us of the same: "Let your 'yes' be yes, and your 'no,' no, or you will be condemned" (James 5:12).

How is it possible to live sexual lives based on God's Word? Only through Christ Jesus. Romans 8:32 rings true: "He who did not spare His own Son, but gave Him up for us all—how will He not also, along with Him, graciously give us all things?" Especially in matters of sex!

Family Planning

CHAPTER 6

He spilled his semen on the ground to keep from producing offspring. (Genesis 38:9)

One of the major questions couples discuss in premarital counseling, as well as among themselves, is "How many children, if any, should we have and when should we have them?" In years past, this question was seldom asked. Children were simply born without much discussion or planning. Statistics tell us that the average couple today has 2.1 children. This is far below the number from the early part of the 1950s, when women were having an average of 3.7 children each. This period in history was called the "baby boom."

Today couples have more choices about having children than they did centuries ago. Some couples simply do not want children. You may hear them say something like, "We don't want to bring children into this messed-up world." More couples are deciding to have children when they are older. Couples who choose not to have children are often chided by their parents or other relatives with such questions as, "When are you going to give us a grandbaby?" or "Don't you think it's time to think about having a child? After all, you're not getting any younger."

Though seldom talked about, people throughout history have sought ways of controlling family size. In some ancient cultures, different substances were inserted into the vagina in hopes that they would prevent conception. Still today, some women ingest the seeds of the Queen Anne's lace plant as an attempt to prevent pregnancy. Today there are a large variety of options available for those who choose to remain childless or who simply want to better plan when and how many children they have.

> "Six in ten pregnancies in the
> United States are unplanned."[1]

As Christian couples discuss whether or not they want children, how many and when, they need to turn to the one parent who knows all things, who is all-wise, who is perfect in His timing—God Himself. "If any of you lacks wisdom, he should ask God, who gives generously to all without finding fault, and it will be given to him" (James 1:5). There are a number of things every couple should remember when making the decision to have children or remain childless:

1. A couple should not have a child because of pressure exerted on them by well-meaning relatives.

2. A couple should not have a child in order to save a marriage that's on the rocks.

3. A couple should prayerfully consider all the obligations (physical, emotional, spiritual) that parenthood entails.

4. A couple should commit themselves to being good stewards of any child God entrusts to them.

5. A couple who choose to remain childless should ask why and make sure that their decision is made only after much prayer and discussion together.

One thing is for certain: If couples wait for the "right time" to have children, such a time may never come. Certainly, before having children, it is important that a newly married couple take time to adjust to each other's uniqueness. They will also want to consider their career goals, finances, and the stability of their marriage. However, despite the best-laid plans, an unexpected pregnancy can occur. If so, a couple will cling to God's promise, "He who did not spare His own Son, but gave Him up for us all—how will He not also, along with Him, graciously give us all things?" (Romans 8:32). Life is life, expected or not; it is a gift to be welcomed with joy.

"For My thoughts are not your thoughts,
  neither are your ways My ways,"
  declares the LORD.
"As the heavens are higher than the earth,
  so are My ways higher than your ways
  and My thoughts than your thoughts."

(Isaiah 55:8–9)

Part of good stewardship is to examine the many different birth-control options available to a couple and decide, based on personal beliefs and opinions, which methods are safest, most effective, and convenient to use. However, no decision should be made without continuously going to the Word of God and kneeling before Him in prayer to ask for wisdom and direction: "The prayer of a righteous man is powerful and effective" (James 5:16).

There are a variety of methods of birth control available today. They fall into five main categories:

1. Periods of Abstinence

2. Barrier Methods

3. Hormonal Methods

4. Sterilization

5. Abortion

Periods of Abstinence

Periods of abstinence, or natural family planning, has traditionally been a method advocated by the Roman Catholic church. It is also called the "rhythm method" because most women have a certain rhythm, or pattern, to their menstrual cycle. A woman determines this pattern in one of four ways: (1) through the calendar method, usually reliable if the woman is "regular," meaning her cycle is predictable each month; (2) through the basal body temperature method, where the woman uses a high-resolution thermometer to indicate the rise in her temperature that tells when ovulation has begun; (3) through checking her cervical mucus, which thins out before ovulating to make it easier for the sperm to travel to its destination; (4) through the sympto-thermal method, which is a combination of all three of the above methods. Though natural family planning has worked for many people, it is one of the least reliable ways of birth control because there are many factors that can break the rhythm of a woman's menstrual cycle, such as undue stress, lack of sleep, vaginal infection, etc.

Barrier Methods

Barrier methods include all the ways in which objects are used to block the sperm from getting to the egg. Some of the more commonly used objects include

1. the diaphragm;

2. the cervical cap;

3. the male condom;

4. the female condom;

5. foams, creams, gels, and sponges.

The Diaphragm

The diaphragm is a latex rubber disk with a flexible rim that is placed into the vagina and over the cervix (see diagram). Users often coat it with a spermicidal jelly or cream before inserting it into the vagina. The diaphragm should initially be fitted by a physician or a nurse in order to assure a correct fit. It must be left in for six to eight hours after intercourse.

Cervical Cap

The cervical cap is much like the diaphragm in that it also fits over the cervix; however, the cap is much smaller. It resembles a thimble. Once inserted, it stays in place by suction. There are disadvantages to the cervical cap, the primary one being that it can be dislodged during lovemaking. It is also not always easy to remove from the cervix.

The Male Condom

A condom is a soft, flexible sheath placed over the man's penis in order to block sperm from entering the vagina (see diagram). Condoms are sold, rolled up, in packages. When placed on the erect penis, the

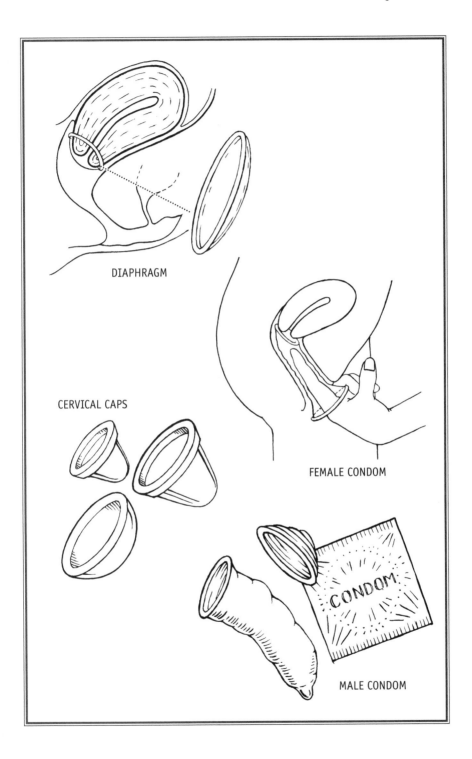

DIAPHRAGM

CERVICAL CAPS

FEMALE CONDOM

MALE CONDOM

condom is rolled down the shaft, a small pocket is left at the top for the deposit of semen.

Because of AIDS, condoms are no longer found only behind drug-store counters or in men's rest rooms. They are now available almost everywhere, including gas stations and supermarkets. Five-year-olds hear about them on television and radio. Because some men claim condoms diminish their pleasure, advertisers try to convince them that their brand is "thinner," provides a "snugger fit," or actually enhances instead of taking away pleasure due to some special lubricant on it. Condoms come in a variety of colors and materials. Most condoms are made out of a synthetic material called latex. Some are made out of animal products. Some are lubricated, others aren't. They are also available in different sizes.

Condoms have disadvantages and, despite what advertisers may say, do not always provide for "safe sex." If the man loses his erection before the removal of a condom, there is always a chance of sperm leakage. Because condoms can slip off or break during intercourse, they do not always protect one from pregnancy or from STDs. Most studies show that there is a failure rate ranging from two to five percent.

The Female Condom

Though it is not heard of very often, a female condom or vaginal pouch has also been developed. It is a lubricated, loose-fitting pouch that is inserted into the vagina (see diagram). The condom has rings at both ends, with one ring being closed. When inserted into the vagina, the closed end is placed at the back of the vagina and over the cervix, while the open-ended ring rests over the vulva area.

Because most female condoms are made of polyurethane, they are safer than men's condoms made out of latex. But just as in the use of the diaphragm and the cervical cap, the open-ended part of the condom can be dislodged by intercourse, allowing semen leakage.

Foams, Creams, Gels, and Sponges

Certain products have been developed that offer a combination of barrier and spermicides which destroy sperm. These spermicidal chemicals are found in the form of creams, foams, jellies and saturated sponges. They can be purchased without prescription. Unfortunately, these spermicides have not always proven to be very reliable in preventing pregnancy.

Hormonal Methods

Various organs in the body are controlled by hormones. By controlling these hormones, especially those that work directly with reproductive organs, pregnancy can often be prevented.

The Birth Control Pill

The birth control pill was in large part responsible for the sexual revolution of the 1960s. Most birth control pills contain a combination of progestin and estrogen. When combined, these two hormones keep the ovaries from releasing eggs. Progestin, a synthetic duplication of the female hormone progesterone, changes the chemical makeup of the cervical mucus, preventing sperm from easily passing into the uterus. It also creates an atmosphere in the uterine lining that makes it difficult for implantation of a fertilized egg. Most birth control pills must be taken every day throughout the 28-day menstrual cycle.

More recently, there has been evidence that the pill has positive side effects other than the prevention of pregnancy. They have proven to help regulate a woman's periods, lessen menstrual cramping and flow, lessen rheumatoid arthritis, and even lower the risk of ovarian cysts and cancer. Though years ago, because of the high dosage of these hormones, birth control pills had been rumored to cause cancer, no real evidence was ever given to prove it, and, in fact, now with the more careful dosage control, the pill may actually prevent cancer.

There has been much research done in the area of creating a male birth control pill. It would work using the same principle as the female pill, except a synthetic version of testosterone, the male hormone, would be used in order to stop the production of sperm. However, because of its present side effects, there is still no such pill available.

Norplant

In 1990 the use of the first birth control implant was approved. Small plastic tubes filled with levonorgestrel, a form of progestin, are inserted just under the skin of a woman's arm. Levonorgestrel prevents ova from being released. It also thickens the cervical mucus, which keeps the sperm from penetrating the uterus. The tubes are the size of match sticks. These implants last up to five years in preventing pregnancy. The obvious advantage is that birth control is not dependent on a daily pill or correctly using a condom. The implants cost from $750 to $1,000 and must be inserted and removed by a medical professional.

Depo-Provera

Instead of taking a pill every day, or inserting birth control implants, another birth control option for women is that of receiving an injection of a long-acting progestin every 12 weeks. This method is known as Depo-Provera. It creates an atmosphere that makes the uterus uninviting for any implantation of the embryo. This method is relatively new in the United States. Some side effects have been reported, such as weight gain and mood swings.

IUD (The Intrauterine Device)

During the sexually permissive days of the '60s and '70s, the intrauterine device was popular. An IUD, or the intrauterine device, is a small, plastic T-shaped device that is inserted into the uterus (see diagram). It has a nylon thread attached to the end, which is left hanging into the vagina so that the woman can check to make sure the IUD is in place. There are presently two types available: (1) one called the Copper T that is plastic with copper wound around it; (2) another called the progestasert, which releases a synthetic hormone called progestin. Both types must be inserted by a medical professional.

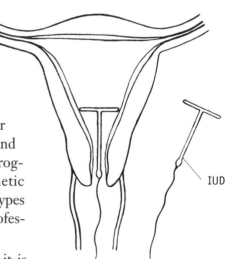

IUD

Even after years of research, it is still unclear how an intrauterine device prevents pregnancy. Most experts have concluded that it either prevents the fertilization of the egg or it keeps the fertilized egg from implanting in the uterus. Depending on which type is used, IUDs can work effectively for one to eight years (the one containing progestin for one year and the one containing copper for eight years).

The Dalkon Shield Controversy

A controversy arose over one IUD commonly used in the 1970s called the Dalkon Shield. Shortly after it was introduced, users complained about complications, especially pelvic inflammatory disease. The problem was that the string attached to the IUD was serving as a conduit for bacteria. Because of thousands of lawsuits, the Dalkon Shield was removed from the market. The controversy also caused great suspicion over many of the other IUDs available, explaining why they are no longer widely used as a contraceptive.

Sterilization

The most common method of birth control for married couples has become voluntary surgical contraception (VSC), or sterilization. The method for women is called *tubal ligation;* for men, *vasectomy.*

Tubal Ligation

Tubal ligation is a process by which the fallopian tubes are cut and tied (see diagram). This prevents sperm from reaching the egg that normally moves from the tube to the uterus. The procedure is relatively simple. It is usually done by a method called *laparoscopy,* in which a small fiber optic scope is inserted through the abdomen. Upon locating the tubes, the doctor uses an instrument to cut and tie the tubes.

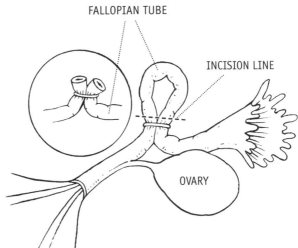

FALLOPIAN TUBE

INCISION LINE

OVARY

The procedure is highly effective in preventing pregnancy. In only about five out of 1,000 cases, the tubes grow back together, allowing impregnation to occur. However, it is one of the safest and best ways of birth control. The cost can range from $2,000 to $3,500.

Vasectomy

In a vasectomy, the vas deferens is cut and tied (see diagram). This prevents the sperm of the male testes from getting into the upper part of the vas deferens. The sperm is still produced but, instead of being ejaculated, it is absorbed by the body. Vasectomies are highly successful in preventing pregnancy. Only two out of 1,000 men find that the tubes grow back together. The surgery is relatively inexpensive in comparison to sterilization for the woman. The cost is approximately $200 to $500 and can be done in about half an hour. Over the years some men have decided to reverse their vasectomies and, with advanced technology, have been able to do so with some success.

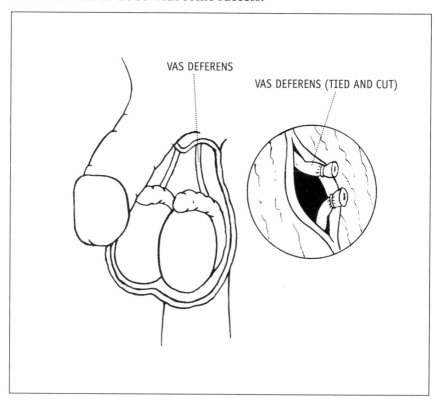

VAS DEFERENS

VAS DEFERENS (TIED AND CUT)

The Top 10 Misconceptions about Birth Control

1. You can't get pregnant the first time you have sexual intercourse.

2. You can't get pregnant if the male does not ejaculate.

3. You can't get pregnant if the female doesn't have an orgasm.

4. You can't get pregnant if a woman is menstruating.

5. You can't get pregnant if you take a shower immediately after sexual intercourse.

6. You can't get pregnant if you stand up while having sexual intercourse.

7. You can't get pregnant if you douche immediately after having sexual intercourse.

8. You can't get pregnant while nursing a newborn.

9. You can't get pregnant if you use a condom.

10. You can't get pregnant if the male doesn't insert his penis into the woman's vagina.

Abortion

One social issue that deeply divides people is abortion. Abortion is the termination of pregnancy before birth. There are two types of abortion: (1) a spontaneous abortion (miscarriage), which is a natural end of the pregnancy; and (2) an elective abortion, which is the surgical or medical termination of a pregnancy.

"Guilt about abortions was not invented by the Pope. Post-abortion trauma is not the dastardly creation of the Moral Majority to punish believers and nonbelievers alike for having killed their unborn children. Guilt and post-abortion trauma are subjects of virtually all feminist literature dealing with termination of pregnancies. You find guilt and post-abortion trauma in non-Christian societies as well as in Judeo-Christian cultures."[2]

On January 22, 1973, the U.S. Supreme Court, in the *Roe* v. *Wade* decision, declared, by a ruling of 7 to 2, that "legal personhood does not exist prenatally." It declared unconstitutional all state laws that protected preborn children from abortion. Essentially it allowed any woman to have an abortion in the first two trimesters (first six months of pregnancy) without any reason, and in the third trimester (last three months) with any reason. Though this ruling has been challenged, it has repeatedly been upheld. From the time of the decision, approximately 1.5 million children have been aborted each year in the U.S. This represents approximately one-third of all pregnancies.

The Use of Fetal Tissue to Save the Lives of Others

Soon after the legalization of abortion, researchers began experimenting with tissues from aborted fetuses to help treat certain diseases. Many conjecture that fetal tissue might be helpful in treating everything from Alzheimer's disease to epilepsy. Though the research has come under criticism by many, it continues to be aided by millions of dollars from federal funds.

"Any principle accepted for the beginning of life will logically be applied by the Courts to the end of life. If private citizens can terminate the life of one human being at the beginning, some will claim the same right to terminate the life of another at the end. Some lower courts have already affirmed this right. The practice of abortion will inure minds and hearts to the practice of mercy killing. The delivery of death by private persons at the beginning of life will lead to the delivery of death by private persons at the end."[3]

From the Perspective of Scripture

Some claim abortion is solely a decision between a woman and her physician. Still others feel that it's really a issue of a preborn child's right to live. For many the argument for or against abortion comes down to the question, "When does life begin, at conception, or at birth, or at some point in between?" The two sides come to radically opposing conclusions to the question.

For the Christian, the answer is not to be found in the laws of the land. It is to be found in the Word of God.

Though the Bible does not offer any explicit statement that life begins at a certain point, it does assume a continuity of life from before the time of birth to after the time of birth. The same language and the same personal pronouns are used indiscriminately for both stages. Further, God's involvement in the life of the person extends back to conception (and even before conception).[4]

Throughout the Old and New Testaments, God attributes the same characteristics to those out of the womb as He does to those within the womb. In this case, it is clear that God's injunction of Exodus 20:13 needs to be heeded in every way: "You shall not murder."

This is most vividly seen in Job 3:3: "May the day of my birth perish, and the night it was said, 'A boy is born!'" The Hebrew word for 'born' is *geber*, which means, literally, "a man-child is conceived." In other words, there wasn't just a "blob of tissue" at conception, there was a boy.

Another passage of importance is Jeremiah 1:5, where it is clear that God refers to the unborn as He refers to a child or adult: "Before I formed you in the womb I knew you, before you were born I set you apart; I appointed you as a prophet to the nations." God was already referring to Jeremiah as a prophet before he was born!

In his psalms, David makes it clear that a growing fetus in the womb is a human being who is "wonderfully" being worked on and loved by God (Psalm 139:13–16). In Psalm 51:5, David clarifies how human he was even before he was born: "Surely I was sinful at birth, sinful from the time my mother conceived me." David bore what all humans bear—a fallen nature. He had this characteristic at conception, into adulthood and old age.

In the New Testament, the word *baby* is used to describe the fetus in Elizabeth's womb: "When Elizabeth heard Mary's greeting, the baby leaped in her womb" (Luke 1:41). Again, the baby was not just some blob of tissue.[5]

Though for many the core issue in abortion is the question of when life begins, the more important issue might be one of sanctity of life. In the Judeo-Christian community, the sanctity of life historically has been upheld. It is obvious why when one scans the first few pages of the book of Genesis. In creating people, God set humans apart from animals. He created them in His very image (Genesis 1:26–27). How much more dignity could He have given them?

> *What is man that You are mindful of him,*
>   *the son of man that You care for him?*
> *You made him a little lower than the heavenly beings*
>   *and crowned him with glory and honor.*
> *You made him ruler over the works of Your hands;*
>   *You put everything under his feet." (Psalm 8:4–6)*

Even after our first parents rebelled against God, after they had sinned, God loved His created beings. If there is any doubt about how important humans are, Jesus' death and resurrection clarifies it for us. Humans were important enough for God to offer up "His one and only Son, that whoever believes in Him shall not perish but have eternal life" (John 3:16). Throughout the New Testament, the proclamation is the same, life is important, all of life.

When There's an Unexpected Pregnancy

Lloyd and Darlene were in their late 40s when they discovered Darlene was pregnant. They already had four children and, though they practiced a form of birth control, they were confident that Darlene was past her child-bearing years. When the pregnancy was confirmed by the doctor, Darlene was afraid, afraid even to tell her husband. Over the years she had heard stories that older women often have babies born with Down's syndrome or with some other birth defect. Darlene did tell Lloyd and, after much prayer and counseling with their pastor, they faced the pregnancy with joy. When the doctor recommended an amniocentesis test, where the fetal cells in the amniotic fluid are tested for signs of birth defects, they agreed to have the test. They also made it clear to their doctor, however, that termination of the pregnancy was not an option for them, despite how the test might turn out.

Darlene was among the 43 percent of women in the United States who discover they have an unintended pregnancy. These women have one of three options to choose from:

1. termination of the pregnancy through abortion
2. placing the child through adoption
3. parenting the baby

Once again, for Lloyd and Darlene termination of the pregnancy through abortion was not an option. Even though financially they were not in a position to have another child, they chose to parent the baby. In doing so, they immediately began to make adequate preparations for the child's health through effective prenatal care as well as to prepare for the child's delivery. Though Lloyd had heard of couples taking Lamaze classes, he had never been in the delivery room during the birth of his other four children. This would be his first time, and he looked forward to it.

 Lamaze, named after the French doctor Fernand Lamaze, is a technique used to help with the delivery of a baby. It usually involves both parents and is a technique of breathing exercises used during the different stages of labor.

Adoption

Though adoption used to be an option chosen by many expectant mothers, today—because of the availability of abortion—very few mothers place their babies for adoption. Because less than five percent of expectant mothers choose to have their children adopted, many infertile couples are left childless.

There are a number of contributing factors, other than abortion, as to why adoption is not as popular as it used to be. Even when talking about adoption, comments such as "giving up a child" have negative connotations to many mothers. More and more adoption agencies, however, are offering mothers the option of staying in contact with the child and adoptive parents.

Over the years, cases such as Baby Jessica (see next page) have also frightened potential adoptive parents. This has caused some couples to go outside the United States for adoption. Their thinking is that mothers who relinquish their children overseas are less likely to come seeking the child later on. There are now lawyers and adoptive agencies throughout the United States who specialize in such adoptions.

The Story of Baby Jessica

In 1993 the story about a little girl named Jessica touched the world. Relinquished by her biological mother at the time of birth, Jessica lived for two years with Jan and Roberta DeBoer, a printer and a homemaker, who treated her as their daughter while they tried to finalize their adoption of her. Then the Michigan Supreme Court ruled that Jan and Roberta DeBoer had to give Jessica back to Dan and Cara Schmidt, the biological parents.

The story affected more than the two sets of parents involved directly. It affected thousands of adoptive parents in the U.S., too. They wondered whether their adopted children might be taken from their homes by a seemingly insensitive legal social services system. For the thousands considering adoption, fear made them step back and ask whether they wanted to risk such terrible grief.[6]

Couples who seek to adopt need to be aware that it can be frustrating and, at times, disappointing. The average cost of an adoption ranges from approximately $12,000 to $25,000. Though some adoptions, such as overseas adoptions, can be done in a relatively short time (a year or less), most of them take much longer. Couples have been known to wait for up to 10 years. Another important factor is the age of the parents. Some agencies will not accept couples who are over a certain age.

When Our Best-Laid Plans Don't Work

Whenever a couple plans their family, they should strive together to reach a decision that is in accordance with God's will. God's will is clearly seen in only one way, through His Word. When one is confused about what the Word might say, it is important that counsel be sought from wise Christian leaders, such as pastors and therapists.

Whenever a couple decides to use a certain birth control method, they should proceed knowing that, even with the best-laid plans, a pregnancy can result. When it does, though it may surprise the couple and trigger some fear, they should remember that God's "thoughts are not [their] thoughts, neither are [His] ways [their] ways" (Isaiah 55:8). When the miracle of birth does occur, the child should be as fully accepted and loved as if he or she had been a result of plans carefully laid for pregnancy to occur.

CHAPTER 7 — Reproduction

God blessed them and said to them, "Be fruitful and increase in number; fill the earth and subdue it." (Genesis 1:28)

It is clear from Scripture and the way He created humans that God intended them to procreate, to reproduce. In fact, He tells us that children are a blessing and need to be seen as such: "Sons are a heritage from the LORD, children a reward from Him. Like arrows in the hands of a warrior are sons born in one's youth. Blessed is the man whose quiver is full of them" (Psalm 127:3–4).

Two of the best gifts God gives to Christian couples are faith and children, and both are miracles. Just as saving faith is totally a gift from God to us, so are our children. Though we express our faith with our words, it is the Holy Spirit working within us that makes such expression possible. Though we are the ones who engaged in lovemaking, it is God who puts within each lover the very creative substances that make conception possible.

> "The reproduction of mankind is a great marvel and mystery. Had God consulted me in the matter, I should have advised him to continue the generation of the species by fashioning them of clay."[1]

The Miracle of Conception

The writers of the psalms in the Old Testament would often break out in praise as they meditated on God's mercy and love. As David thought of his deliverance from his enemies, he could not help but exclaim, "His love endures forever" (Psalm 118:2, 3, 4). The same exclamation is ours as we consider the miracle of conception. Review just a few of the details of this marvelous creative process:

1. Each ovary contains a quarter of a million egg cells, placed there by God even before the woman is born. These eggs each contain 23 chromosomes, the woman's genetic contribution to new life. During the woman's menstrual cycle, hormones usually stimulate the growth of a single one of these eggs (ovum). The follicle around the egg ruptures and the ovary releases the egg into a fallopian tube: this is called *ovulation*.

2. The egg enters the fallopian tube and travels toward the uterus. Upon meeting with the sperm, the egg is fertilized. Though there are literally millions of sperm attempting to find the egg, only one penetrates it. Once it does, an immediate covering envelopes the egg, blocking the entry of any other sperm. The now-fertilized egg is called a zygote.

3. The sperm brings with it the same number of chromosomes as the egg does—23—each containing genes stored in the form of DNA, deoxyribonucleic acid. The 23 maternal chromosomes and the 23 paternal chromosomes form 22 matching pairs of non-sex chromosomes which are called *autosomes* and one pair that determines the future sex of the child (XX or XY). It is the sperm that carries the sex-determining chromosome.

4. After fertilization, the zygote continues to divide over and over, growing continually over the three to four days it takes it to move toward the uterus. When it reaches the uterus, it attaches itself to the nutrient rich lining there. Then it continues to grow for 266 days, or approximately 9 months.

5. During the first few weeks, the fertilized egg takes root in the upper part of the uterus. As it grows, it forms into what is called an *embryo*. As the outer cells of the embryo spread into the lining of the uterus, a mass forms called the *placenta*, later called the *afterbirth*. The placenta connects the mother and the baby. It is literally the baby's life-support, because it not only supplies food and oxygen to the baby

but it also discards its waste products. A cord called the *umbilical cord* connects the baby to the placenta.

6. During pregnancy, a baby floats in a sac of amniotic fluid. This fluid protects and cushions the newly forming life. The fluid remains fresh most of the time because it is continually being replenished by the mother every six hours. This amniotic fluid also helps regulate the baby's temperature. Just before birth, the sac holding the fluid breaks, warning the expectant parents that birth is imminent. Then they know they'd better head for the hospital if they're not already there!

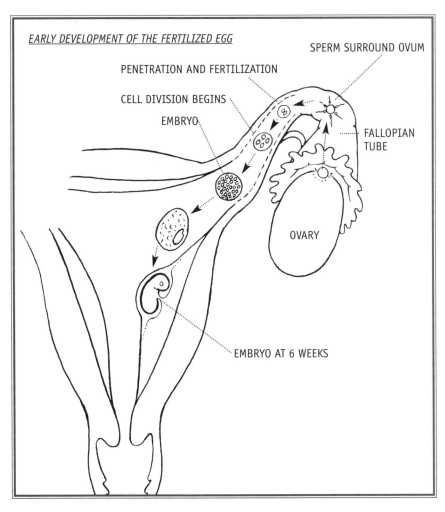

EARLY DEVELOPMENT OF THE FERTILIZED EGG

SPERM SURROUND OVUM

PENETRATION AND FERTILIZATION

CELL DIVISION BEGINS

EMBRYO

FALLOPIAN TUBE

OVARY

EMBRYO AT 6 WEEKS

Ectopic Pregnancy

An ectopic pregnancy occurs when the fetus develops outside the uterus, usually in the fallopian tube. Ectopic pregnancies can lead to the death of the mother and baby if not surgically removed.

Twins—How Does It Happen?

The birth of twins is now occurring more than years ago, in part because of the use of fertility drugs, which stimulate the ovaries to release more than one egg.

Fraternal twins do not look alike and may not even be the same sex, because they are the result of two different eggs fertilized by two separate spermatozoa.

Identical twins are the result of one egg fertilized by one sperm. The egg then splits into two. This results in two babies of the same sex and appearance.

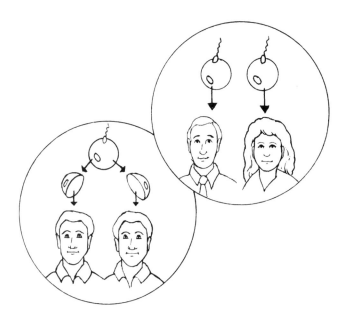

The Growth of the Baby Month-by-Month

The miracle of life doesn't stop with conception. For approximately nine months, a new life grows and develops in the mother's womb. Not only is God forming the child's fingers and toes, inserting the exact number of hairs on his or her head, and determining the child's future height, He is also making plans for his or her future.

> *Before I formed you in the womb I knew you, before you were born I set you apart; I appointed you as a prophet to the nations. (Jeremiah 1:5)*

> *When I was woven together in the depths of the earth, Your eyes saw my unformed body. All the days ordained for me were written in Your book before one of them came to be. (Psalm 139:15–16)*

Though we call the fertilized egg for the first eight weeks of pregnancy an *embryo* and after that a *fetus*, it does not minimize the fact that it is a human life, nor does it minimize the urgency of preserving that life at all costs. For life—all of it, from conception to death—is protected under God's Law. And in the United States, notwithstanding the Supreme Court Decision of *Roe* v. *Wade*, the Declaration of Independence declares that "all men are created [not born] equal, that they are endowed by their Creator with certain unalienable Rights," the first of which is life. As we review the miracle of life growing in the mother's womb, we once again are compelled to exclaim with the psalmist, "Great is the LORD, and most worthy of praise" (Psalm 48:1).

First Month

• A simple brain, spine, and central nervous system begin to form.

• The legs and arms begin to grow.

• Both the circulatory and the digestive systems begin to form.

Second Month

• Noticeable spots can be seen where the eyes, nose, and mouth will be.

• The heart begins to beat at about 140–50 pulses per minute.

• The major organs are beginning to form.

The Third Month

• The toes and fingers are now in position.

- Ears and earlobes begin to develop.
- The baby is opening and shutting his mouth.
- Teeth buds are beginning to form.
- Vocal cords are developing.
- Blood circulation is beginning.
- Both the liver and the kidneys are beginning to function.
- The baby begins to move, even kick at times.
- Her fingers close to form a fist.
- The male penis or female vulva are beginning to form.

The Fourth Month

- The body and its vital organs are for the most part formed.
- The baby may suck his thumb.
- The baby hears sounds.
- Hair is growing on the baby's head, along with eyelashes and eyebrows.
- The baby yawns, swallows, gets the hiccups.

The Fifth Month

- Her teeth buds are beginning to grow.
- Facial features such as wrinkles are appearing.
- Hair, called *lanugo*, covers most of the baby's body.
- A lubricant called *vernix* covers the skin.

Are Lanugo and Vernix Some Tropical Diseases or What?
After six months the preborn baby is completely covered with a furry covering of hair called *lanugo*. By the time the baby is born, he or she has, however, shed most of this hair. These hairs serve to retain the protective ointment called *vernix* that is secreted from special glands surrounding the hair follicles. The lubricant is greasy and white in color. It coats the entire body of the baby. As with everything, there is a reason for this protective covering. It prevents the baby from getting irritating and dangerous skin infections due to urine in the amniotic fluid the baby is swimming in. Vernix also provides lubrication for easier delivery.

The Sixth Month

- The baby is capable of fighting off disease and infection.
- The baby is becoming more and more active.
- Creases are appearing on the fingers.
- Fingerprints and toe prints are visible.

The Seventh Month

- Taste buds are forming.
- Signs of a personality are beginning to show.
- Though the branches of the baby's lungs continue to develop, they will only be fully developed after the baby is born.
- The baby opens his eyes and looks around at his home called the womb.
- The amount of amniotic fluid is decreasing.

Before John the Baptist was born, he expressed emotion—leaping within his mother's womb—upon being in the presence of the Messiah, according to Luke 1:41–44:

> When Elizabeth heard Mary's greeting, the baby leaped in her womb, and Elizabeth was filled with the Holy Spirit. In a loud voice she exclaimed: "Blessed are you among women, and blessed is the child you will bear! But why am I so favored, that the mother of my Lord should come to me? As soon as the sound of your greeting reached my ears, the baby in my womb leaped for joy."

The Eighth Month

- The baby is hearing distinct sounds and is responding, especially upon hearing her mother's or father's voice.
- The baby is developing a layer of cells that line the air sacs within the lungs. These cells produce *surfactant*, a substance that keeps the newborns lungs from collapsing after birth.

The Ninth Month

- The lanugo hair and some of the vernix disappears.
- There is rapid growth of the brain.

- Toe nails and fingernails are now covering the baby's toes and fingers.
- Fat cells are being deposited under the baby's skin to help regulate his temperature upon birth.
- The baby's head is pressing harder each day against the pelvis.

The Average Weight and Length of a Baby During Pregnancy

First Month: ⅒ of an inch long and weighing in at ? (about the size of a small grain of rice!).

Second Month: One inch long and weighing in at ⅓ of an ounce.

Third Month: Two inches long and weighing in at about ½ ounce.

Fourth Month: Six inches long and weighing in at about 7 ounces.

Fifth Month: Ten inches long and weighing in at about 12 ounces.

Sixth Month: Fourteen inches long and weighing in at about 1 pound, 4 ounces.

Seventh Month: Fifteen inches long and weighing in at about 2 pounds and 11 ounces.

Eight Month: Sixteen inches long and weighing in at about 4 pounds.

Ninth Month: One foot, 6 inches long and weighing in between 6 to 11 pounds.

The Birth Process

Closer to delivery, the baby will shift, head-downward, to the lower part of the mother's abdomen. Just prior to birth, the uterus begins to contract. This is commonly known as "labor pains." During this time, the amniotic sac breaks. Water from the sac begins to exit the vagina. The uterine contractions vary. Though at first they may be only in intervals of every 20 minutes or so, they continue to increase as delivery gets closer. The uterine cervix also dilates to a diameter of approximately 10 centimeters.

The child then moves out of the uterus into the vagina. The vagina now functions as the "birth canal." Normally, the head is the first to appear at the vaginal opening, followed by one shoulder at a time, and then the rest of the body. The time for the entire birth process varies, depending on several factors, including whether or not it is the first delivery for the mother. The actual birthing time, from when the child begins to exit the uterus to when it has passed through the birth canal to the outside of the mother's body, usually takes one to two hours for the mother's first delivery. Subsequent deliveries usually take less time.

Breech Birth
In a "breech birth," the baby's feet or buttocks appear first instead of the head.

Upon delivery, the placenta and the remains of the umbilical cord are also expelled from the uterus. Together, these tissues are called the "afterbirth." This completes the birth process.

There are times when the mother may not be able to safely deliver the baby. When this is the case, a surgical procedure known as a Caesarean section takes place. An incision is made in the abdominal wall and uterus in order to remove the baby. Reasons for such a procedure vary from that of the baby being too large for the woman's pelvis to that of preventing the child from being infected by the mother's STD.

Episiotomy
To make childbirth easier, some doctors do a procedure called an *episiotomy*. The outer part of the vaginal tissue is cut, not only to make delivery easier but to keep the vaginal opening from ripping during delivery. After birth, the incision is sutured.

A Miracle

A miracle is often defined as a supernatural manifestation of divine power in the external world. Such supernatural manifestations were seen often while Jesus lived here on earth, such as when He changed water into wine (John 2:1–11) and when He fed 5,000 people (John 6:1–13). As He performed more and more of these miracles, the crowds of people who sought Him multiplied.

However, Jesus' real purpose for coming was more than to sustain life for a few earthly years or to heal someone of a serious crippling illness. It was to prepare a way for an eternal life with God. It could happen in only one way: through a perfect life on His part in order to fulfill the Law; through His death in order to pay the price we all deserved to pay because of sin; and through a resurrection, providing a resurrection for all people (Galatians 4:4–5; Romans 6:23; Romans 4:25).

In a book by the same title, the authors speak of the "miracle of life" that takes place in the womb of a mother for nine months after conception. They write:

> It was Saint Augustine who said: "We take for granted the slow miracles whereby year by year water irrigating a vineyard becomes wine; we stand amazed when the same process takes place in quick motion in Cana of Galilee."

> What is taking place within the well-irrigated vineyard of your womb is a miracle, but it happens so slowly we take it for granted. After all, nine months is a long time to wait for a miracle.[2]

Though this miracle is not instantaneous, few other miracles even compare to it. The miracle that God produces in the womb of a mother takes place over a period of 266 days or 39 weeks. Eighteen days after conception, until the baby is born, God weaves throughout the baby an intricate network of nerves and muscles that will enable it to do everything from hear to walk. He is forming the eyes, placing in the very back of each one the retina, which will consist of 137 million cells—130 million of them to see black and white and seven million to help see color. The lungs, which begin developing at the fourth month, will end up consisting of a mesh of small blood vessels, called capillaries, that if laid out end to end would stretch out over 1,500 miles.

A careful review of what takes place, day by day, week by week, month by month, shows us only one thing—God is at work. From the way God placed into man and woman the ingredients needed for procreation, to the workings that He carefully orchestrates within the mother's womb during the nine months of pregnancy, a person can only come to one conclusion—human life is a miracle! It is a supernatural manifestation of divine power in the external world.

> "I do not know how you appeared in my womb; it was not I who endowed you with breath and life, I had not the shaping of your every part. It is the creator of the world, ordaining the process of man's birth and presiding over the origin of all things" (2 Maccabees 7:22–23 TJB).

CHAPTER 8   Infertility Advances

"Hannah, why are you weeping? Why don't you eat? Why are you downhearted? Don't I mean more to you than ten sons?" (1 Samuel 1:8)

For years, much of the reproduction research done was in the area of birth control and very little in the area of infertility. The problem of infertility in the U.S. became more acute with the *Roe* v. *Wade* Supreme Court decision, when abortion was declared legal. This ruling meant that over a million children each year would not be available for adoption. Since that time, a host of breakthroughs have been made in the field of infertility. This is good news for the approximately 15 percent of all couples who desire to have children but are unable to conceive. One statistic shows that from 1988 to 1995 infertility had a 25 percent increase. Some suggest that environmental pollutants and chemicals in the food have contributed to the rise; however, another important factor is that more and more couples are choosing to wait until they are older to have children.

"Infertility affects about 5.3 million Americans ... according to the American Society for Reproductive Medicine."[1]

A couple is considered to be infertile after attempting to conceive for one year. Statistics show that up to 90 percent of all sexually active couples will conceive before one year. However, when they are unable to, though the problem may be specifically with the man or the woman, the impact is felt by both. For example, more than half of all couples with infertility problems report a decrease in frequency of intercourse and sexual satisfaction. Making love for them may feel more like "sex on demand" as they try to follow the orders of their doctors on when and how to produce a baby.

Suggestions That Are *Not* Helpful to an Infertile Couple

"Just get away for a week and you'll end up pregnant!"

"If you need some instructions in the bedroom, I'll be happy to assist you."

"Adopt a kid. Then you'll end up having a kid of your own."

"Consider yourself fortunate you don't have any children. Ours have only brought us trouble!"

"Does your husband wear boxers or briefs? Guaranteed, if he wears boxers instead of briefs, you'll have a child in nine months."

"You'd better hurry up and do what you have to do to get pregnant because your biological time clock is running out!"

"At least, I'll bet you you're having a lot of fun trying to have a child."

"Give up some of your work and you'll get pregnant."

"Light some candles ... take a bubble bath together ... give each other a massage."

"Just stop worrying about it."

Infertility problems are evenly divided between men and women. In approximately one-fifth of the cases, both contribute to the infertility, or it is simply impossible to determine the source of the problem.

There are a number of factors that can contribute to a woman's infertility. One of the more common reasons is endometriosis, a condition in which the endometrium, or uterine lining, grows out of the uterus onto surrounding organs. Other reasons include diabetes, hypertension, and pelvic inflammatory disease.

Infertility among males is usually due to a low sperm count or because of slow motility of the sperm. Other reasons include the use of drugs, alcohol, and tobacco, as well as injury to the testes, which can adversely affect the production of sperm.

Whatever the reason for the rising rate of infertility, a host of breakthroughs have been made available to enable infertile couples to have children. These are some of the newer options:

1. fertility drugs
2. in vitro fertilization (IVF)
3. gamete intrafallopian transfer (GIFT)
4. zygote intrafallopian transfer (ZIFT)
5. artificial insemination by the husband (AIH)
6. intracytoplasmic sperm injection (ICSI)
7. artificial insemination by a donor (AID)
8. donor egg
9. surrogate motherhood

Fertility Drugs

It was a fertility drug that Bobbi McCaughey from Carlisle, Iowa, took in 1997 that, in her second pregnancy, produced seven children. Their doctor, a reproductive endocrinologist in fertility, had warned the McCaugheys that Metrodin, the fertility drug prescribed to her, could cause multiple births, but they had no idea how many until one day an ultrasound was taken. Encased in Mrs. McCaughey were seven babies, each in their own tiny sac of amniotic fluid. Though multiple pregnancies often end in miscarriage or stillbirth, Bobbi McCaughey carried the babies to viability and, in November of 1997, the population of Carlisle, Iowa, increased by seven.

There are a variety of fertility drugs other than Metrodin. One of the more popular ones is clomiphene citrate (Clomid, Serophene), which, through the stimulation of the hypothalamus and the pituitary, increases stimulation of the ovaries to produce mature eggs. For those women who do not respond to clomiphene, menopausal gonadotropin (Pergonal) is prescribed. Unlike clomiphene, Pergonal directly stimulates the ovaries to produce eggs.

In Vitro Fertilization (IVF)

Research began in the '60s with "in vitro fertilization" (IVF). The words *in vitro* literally mean "in glass," because the fertilization takes place outside the woman's body in a glass petri dish. The procedure is threefold: (1) eggs are harvested from the woman and sperm from the man; (2) the eggs and sperm are put together in a petri dish for fertilization; and (3) one of the fertilized eggs is placed into the woman's uterus. The first successful test-tube baby, named Louise Brown, was born in 1978 to a mother in Oldham, England. Since that time, in vitro fertilization has been used to bring about the birth of thousands of babies.

Gamete Intrafallopian Transfer (GIFT)

In "gamete intrafallopian transfer" (GIFT), the sperm and eggs are mixed outside the body and placed in the woman's fallopian tube to fertilize rather than in a sterile dish. By placing a large concentration of sperm cells in the same area, the odds of fertilization increase.

Zygote Intrafallopian Transfer (ZIFT)

In "zygote intrafallopian transfer" (ZIFT). the fertilized egg or zygote is inserted into the woman's fallopian tube. This is done within 24 to 48 hours of fertilization. It requires minor surgery because a laparoscopy is needed in order to transfer the zygotes into the fallopian tube.

Artificial Insemination by Husband (AIH)

There are instances when a husband produces viable sperm, but in insufficient quantities to impregnate his wife. Then, the couple may turn to artificial insemination, where the husband's sperm are harvested, concentrated, and placed in the wife's vagina or uterus during her most fertile time.

Intracytoplasmic Sperm Injection (ICSI)

Another procedure to aid in reproduction is the "direct sperm injection." A large ultrafine needle injects a single sperm into an egg for fertilization. The first child to be born due to this method was in 1993. By isolating sperm, specialists can select those that are most motile.

Artificial Insemination by Donor (AID)

When a husband is unable to produce any adequate sperm for fertilization, sperm is taken from donors and inserted into the woman's body. All donors sign a waiver of parental rights.[2]

Donor Egg

When a woman is unable to produce eggs, the eggs of another woman are harvested. These eggs are then used for fertilization and inserted into the infertile woman's uterus. These eggs may come from a variety of sources, including what are known as "egg banks."

Surrogate Motherhood

When a woman cannot, or chooses not to, carry her own child, the developing embryo may be planted in another woman's uterus. This woman is then known as a "surrogate mother." Major newspapers carry the names of such women who, for a fee, will agree to bear a child for an infertile couple. Throughout its history, the program has raised its share of complications and ethical questions. Some see this practice as nothing more than a means of selling and buying babies.

Distinctions in Surrogate Motherhood

Genetic surrogacy = "the surrogate mother contributes the egg and uterus ... artificially inseminated by the husband of the infertile couple."

Gestational surrogacy = "the surrogate contributes only the uterus with the egg coming from the wife of the infertile couple." The wife's egg is fertilized by her husband's sperm by means of in vitro fertilization, then implanted in the surrogate mother.

Commercial surrogacy = "done for fee"

Altruistic surrogacy = "done by a friend or relative out of the goodness of her heart"[3]

Other Reproduction Options

As infertility research continues, more and more new techniques and procedures are being made available for infertile couples. In one of the newest methods, the fertilized eggs are left to grow in vitro for up to five days, making it possible for the embryologists to pick out one or two of the strongest embryos and then selectively implant them into the uterus.

Though opposed by the majority of people, a team of doctors are beginning to accept couples for what is known as embryo cloning, meaning the duplication of an embryo that has been previously fertilized in vitro in the lab. "They reproduced in the lab the same process that occurs in the body where identical twins (or triplets) are produced."[4]

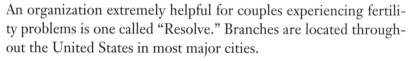

An organization extremely helpful for couples experiencing fertility problems is one called "Resolve." Branches are located throughout the United States in most major cities.

Resolve
1310 Broadway
Somerville, MA
92144-1131
(617-623-0744)

Ethical Issues

There are many ethical and moral issues raised by the reproductive and fetal technologies now available for infertile couples. For example, these new technologies now help women defy their own biological clocks, enabling them to become pregnant beyond the years of what was once considered possible. The question raised by some is, "Are we playing around with God's time clock and, if so, is it right?" Or what about the time when a true "test-tube baby" is produced, meaning it spends its entire prenatal time outside of the human body. What about the procedure where an older egg's less reliable cellular components are bypassed and replaced with the DNA components of a younger one, a process known as a DNA Transfer? Will embryonic cloning deprive an individual the right to have his or her own identity? More importantly, what does God say about any of these procedures in His Word?

One Church's Statement of Belief

In the 1980s a standing committee of the Division of Theological Studies of the Lutheran Council in the U.S.A., after a two-year discussion, published its findings. … While The Lutheran Church—Missouri Synod has not established an official position on IVF, the participants from the LCMS concurred: "IVF does not *in and of itself* violate the will of God as reflected in the Bible, when the wife's egg and the husband's sperm are used." The LCMS participants concluded that IVF is unobjectionable however, only when it is carried out subject to two limitations:

"a. Because the Biblical injunction to be fruitful and multiply was given by God to a man and a woman united in the one-flesh union of marriage … only the sperm and the eggs of a man and woman united in marriage may be employed. Any use of donor sperm or eggs involves the intrusion of a third party into the one-flesh union and is contrary to the will of God. For the same reason surrogate wombs may not be used.

"b. Because the unborn are persons in God's sight from the time of conception … *all* fertilized eggs must be returned to the womb of the woman. Any experimentation with, destruction of, or storage of unneeded or defective fertilized eggs fails to accord respect and reverence for new life brought into being by God at the moment of conception and is, therefore, contrary to His will. The same considerations preclude any required agreement of the woman to permit the interruption of an IVF pregnancy for any reason other than to prevent her death.[5] "

Some would suggest that we have no right to play around at all with the most basic of biological functions—reproduction of our own. Though some of the practices now available, such as using the egg or the sperm of another woman or man to make pregnancy possible, would raise some serious ethical questions for most Christians, other methods would be perfectly acceptable and in no way contrary to God's Word.

Many of the procedures now available only help put things back to the way things were before sin entered the world. Sin mixed things up. It turned things upside down. Things that were once normal and easy—to "be fruitful and increase in number"—became difficult or impossible. The created and the creation were both gravely affected; "For the creation was subjected to frustration ... We know that the whole creation has been groaning as in the pains of childbirth right up to the present time" (Romans 8:20a, 22).

Those involved in helping make babies possible for infertile couples are really nothing more than "facilitators, trying, essentially, to put things back to the way they work in nature," people being used by God to help re-assemble things and put them back into order again.[6] The wisest reproductive doctors, the most learned geneticists, cannot produce offspring. Only God can produce life. The rest of us are merely servants being used to facilitate and carry out His plans.

Moving On

Surveys have shown that infertility can place a tremendous strain on marriage. The infertility issue can often uncover or magnify other problems in a marriage. As one couple lamented, "This baby business has taken over our lives. All we ever talk about is having a baby."

There comes a time when a couple can no longer think about temperature charts, the timing of sexual intercourse, or take one more emotional roller coaster ride with another procedure, only to discover pregnancy did not occur. The adoption line may seem too long or be something a couple may choose not to enter into. Whenever that time comes, it is important to close the chapter together and move on together. It means making a decision to change one's focus and to make plans for the future that may look somewhat different from the original plan. It will be a time when one stops dwelling on the whys. It will mean praying, perhaps, in a direction different from before. It will mean trusting that even when we can't trace God's ways, we still remember His promise:

"For I know the plans I have for you," declares the LORD, "plans to prosper you and not to harm you, plans to give you hope and a future." (Jeremiah 29:11)

CHAPTER 9

Sexually Transmitted Diseases

For the wages of sin is death, but the gift of God is eternal life in Christ Jesus our Lord. (Romans 6:23)

The one who sows to please his sinful nature, from that nature will reap destruction; the one who sows to please the Spirit, from the Spirit will reap eternal life. (Galatians 6:8)

The pleasures of sin [are] for a short time. (Hebrews 11:25)

There are many things we can learn as we listen and look at what's happening in the world around us. One of the things we can conclude is that God's Word is true. There are consequences for those who live in disobedience to God's Word (Romans 6:23). Unfortunately, when some people suffer from the consequences of their sin, they blame God instead of seeing it as a result of their own sin.

As in Jesus' parable of the lost sheep (Luke 15:1–7), the shepherd was not negligent; the sheep wandered off on their own, but in wandering off, they soon encountered danger. So do humans. God does not coerce His people into obedience. In loving us, He seeks loving obedience on our part. When we wander and live in disobedience, there are consequences. Certainly the consequences of such disobedience are most obvious in the area of sexuality and the many sexually transmitted diseases that millions of people now suffer from.

STDs (Sexually Transmitted Diseases)

The acronym STD stands for a "sexually transmitted disease." (STD is more descriptive than the earlier term, "venereal disease" or VD.) Most sexual diseases are transmitted through the exchange of body fluids. This happens either through vaginal intercourse or outercourse, such as oral or anal sex. Since STD germs cannot exist outside the body, most STDs are not transferred through mere touch or normal signs of affection.

In a survey, it was discovered that only 22 percent of high school students had knowledge of any sexually transmitted diseases other than HIV/AIDS. Though AIDS is certainly a disease that kills and should be known about, the truth of the matter is that there are other STDs that can be just as deadly and destructive. As Christians it is important for us to know what these diseases are as well as the treatments available so that we might lovingly minister and counsel our children and children's children.

"Therefore do not let sin reign in your mortal body so that you obey its evil desires. Do not offer the parts of your body to sin, as instruments of wickedness, but rather offer yourselves to God, as those who have been brought from death to life; and offer the parts of your body to Him as instruments of righteousness. For sin shall not be your master, because you are not under law, but under grace" (Romans 6:12–14).

"My people are destroyed from lack of knowledge." (Hosea 4:6)

"Where there is no revelation, the people cast off restraint; but blessed is he who keeps the law." (Proverbs 29:18)

"For lack of guidance a nation falls, but many advisers make victory sure." (Proverbs 11:14)

Chlamydia

- Up to 25 percent of sexually active college students have chlamydia.
- An estimated four million cases of chlamydia occur in the United States each year.
- Seventy-five percent of women with chlamydia have no visible signs of being infected.

Chlamydia is one of the most common STDs today among college students. Chlamydia is a minute parasite that invades the cells, multiplying within them. It can cause severe damage without the infected person even knowing he or she carries the disease. When there are symptoms, they can include the following things: fever, urethral discharge from the penis or vagina, pain or burning during urination, pain during sexual intercourse or during a bowel movement, swelling in the testicles or cervix, and spotting between menstrual periods.

Symptoms of Chlamydia

Symptoms **Males** *Early Stages*	*Symptoms* **Females** *Early Stages*
Burning sensation during urination	Burning sensation during urination
Discharge of pus from the penis	Pain during intercourse
	Itching in the vulva area
Nausea	Nausea
Fever	Fever
Later Stages	*Later Stages*
Irritation, even pain, in the testicles	Pain in the pelvic and abdominal area
Infertility	Menstrual irregularity
	Infection of the fallopian tubes
	Infertility

Treatment

In its earliest stages, chlamydia can be treated with tetracycline or azithromycin (Zithromax). If the disease infects the fallopian tubes, it is not as easily treatable. The disease scars the tubes and can cause permanent infertility. If a woman has chlamydia during the birth process, her baby has a very high chance of also being infected.

Genital Herpes

- 30 to 35 percent of all unmarried people who are sexually active have been infected with herpes by age 30.
- Approximately 30 million Americans carry the virus.
- Over 500,000 new cases of herpes are reported each year.

Genital herpes is caused by a virus and is most often transmitted through sexual activity. There are two strains of the virus: (1) Type 1 (HSV-1), and (2) Type 2 (HSV-2). Both viruses can be transmitted in a variety of ways including kissing, touching, etc. The disease is highly contagious. An infected person sheds cells of the virus even after the outbreak itself has subsided.

Exposure to the herpes simplex virus-2 (HSV-2) has many dire consequences. If a mother has an active herpes infection during childbirth, the child can incur some serious health problems and developmental disabilities. It can even cause death to the child. Exposure of the virus to one's eyes can cause an infection known as herpes keratitis. Unless treated, it can do severe damage to the cornea. Having genital herpes has also been known to increase one's risk to human immunodeficiency virus (HIV). There is no cure for herpes.

Symptoms of Genital Herpes

Symptoms **Males**	*Symptoms* **Females**
Prickling sensation when blisters begin to appear	Prickling sensation when blisters begin to appear

Blisters and sores on the genitalia and elsewhere on the body	Blisters and sores on the genitalia and elsewhere on the body
Fever	Fever
Headache	Headache
Fatigue	Fatigue
Swollen lymph nodes in groin area	Possible infection and even death for a newborn baby

Treatment

Like all diseases that are virus-generated, there are no known permanent cures. Symptoms can only be relieved. One medication that has proven to be effective is zovirax, either taken in pill form or as an ointment. Acyclovir has also been known to relieve the symptoms of the disease.

Gonorrhea

- One million cases of gonorrhea are reported each year in the United States.
- Approximately 30 percent of people who are infected with gonorrhea are also infected with chlamydia.
- Twenty-five percent of all women who become infected with gonorrhea for a second time become infertile.

Gonorrhea has been around for years. It has been referred to by a variety of slang terms such as "the clap" or "the drip." Its symptoms are similar to the STD known as chlamydia. Gonorrhea is caused by pus-producing bacteria transmitted through sexual contact either by vaginal intercourse, oral sex, or anal sex. The disease can also be transferred by an infected mother to her newborn baby as the baby passes through the birth canal. Since the eyes of the child are most vulnerable to the infection, the obstetrician places antibacterial drops into the child's eyes immediately upon birth to kill any damaging bacteria.

Symptoms of Gonorrhea

Symptoms **Males**	*Symptoms* **Females**
Early Stages	*Early Stages*
Burning sensation in the urethra or during urination	Yellowish discharge from the urethra
Itching in the urethra	Menstruation irregularity
Discharge of pus-like substance from the urethra	Soreness of the throat
	Soreness in the rectum area
	Bowel abnormalities
Later Stages	*Later Stages*
Scarring of the urethra or for semen to pass through	Painful urination that may require cauterization
Infection of the kidneys, prostate, bladder, and testes	Infection of the ovaries, fallopian tubes, uterus, and intestines
Sterility	Inflammation of the pelvis
Complications in the heart and brain	Complications in the heart and brain
	Sterility

Treatment

Many of the new strains of gonorrhea are no longer treatable through the use of penicillin. Now the disease is often treated with a drug called ceftriaxone (Recephin). Other drugs such as ciprofloxacin and cefiximine have also been used successfully for treatment. Newborns of infected mothers have their eyes immediately washed out with a silver nitrate solution.

HIV/AIDS

- One in 100 sexually active adults worldwide are HIV infected.
- Up to 5 percent of all men do not show symptoms of having HIV for 20 years.
- HIV/AIDS is the leading cause of death for men between the ages of 25 and 44 years of age.

The most dreaded and feared of all sexually transmitted diseases is a viral infection called HIV, human immunodeficiency virus, because it leads to Acquired Immune Deficiency Syndrome (AIDS). Though God placed within humans an intricate immune system, the human immunodeficiency virus attacks the cells of the immune system and destroys or weakens its capacity to fight disease. The final stage of HIV infection is known as AIDS. Once infected with the virus, a person is said to be HIV positive.

Infection occurs most commonly through anal or vaginal intercourse, sharing intravenous needles and syringes used for drugs, tattooing, ear piercing, receiving organs of an infected person, and transference from a mother to a child in pregnancy. Although the AIDS virus is highly contagious, it is not transmitted in the same way as an ordinary cold, measles, or chicken pox. It is not spread by kissing or swimming in pools where those with AIDS are swimming. It is not spread by mosquitoes or birds, nor via toilet seats, telephones, books, computer keys, or doorknobs. It is transmitted from semen-to-blood or blood-to-blood contact.

An Ounce of Prevention

Surveys show that despite the voluminous amount of information about AIDS for college students, most of them have not changed their sexual behavior. For example, a survey at the University of Massachusetts found that nearly seven out of 10 students had not changed their sexual practices because of AIDS.[1]

Because a large percentage of the homosexual community engage in anal sex, early in the history of the disease the HIV/AIDS virus spread more rapidly among this group than the heterosexual community. God did not design the anus to be penetrated from the outside and so the anal lining easily rips and bleeds when a penis or some other object is thrust into it. HIV-infected semen or blood from the invading penis easily enters the bloodstream of the recipient.

Though there have been a few reported cases of getting the virus from oral sex, more recent studies have shown that this practice is not as risky as first thought. Needless to say, it is difficult in many cases to know whether or not the virus is passed on through oral sex or some other means, because oral sex is often done in conjunction with other dangerous sexual activity. Theoretically, if the mouth has any minute breaks along the gum line or in the cheeks, it would seem logical that the AIDS virus could enter.

About half of HIV-infected people will begin to show signs within five to six years. Anyone who has been sexually active should be tested for HIV. Early detection can mean earlier treatment in helping the immune system work effectively.

Symptoms of Human Immunodeficiency Virus (HIV/AIDS)

Symptoms	Males and Females
Early Stages	Fever
	Swollen glands
	Rash
	Fatigue
Second Stage	Chronically swollen lymph nodes
	Immune cells that continue to decline
Third Stage	Thrush, a yeast infection of the mouth
	Weight loss
	Night sweats
	Infections of the skin
	AIDS
	Purplish skin lesions
	Pneumonia
	Cancer

Brain and spinal cord damage

Blindness

Dementia

Paralysis

Death

Treatment

Like all diseases that are virus-generated, there are no known permanent cures. Symptoms can only be relieved. One medication, called AZT, azidothymidine, has proven to prolong the patient's life and improve its quality, especially when used with certain other drugs in a mixture known as a "cocktail." The purpose of any treatment is to keep a patient's immune system operating effectively. Because of early detection and treatment, many HIV-infected people are living much longer. It should be noted, however, that there is no cure for HIV/AIDS.

Thirty million people worldwide are infected with the AIDS virus. Each day, nearly 16,000 newly infected are added to that number. This means that one in every 100 sexually active adults worldwide are infected with HIV, with the majority of them not knowing they are infected. Approximately 2.3 million people died of AIDS in 1997, with predictions are that this number will steadily increase each year.

Human Papilloma Virus (HPV) or Genital Warts

- Up to 45 percent of all sexually active single people have human papilloma virus.
- Forty million women and men are infected with the disease.
- There are over 90 known varieties of the disease.

Human papilloma virus causes an infection that is most often transmitted through vaginal, oral, or anal sex. It is one of the most common of all STDs. Though there are over 60 different strains of the disease, types 6, 11, 16, 18, 31, 33, and 35 are the most dangerous. The disease often has no outward symptoms. Symptoms that *may* appear: warts and lesions on the genital area. Each year over one million additional people in the United States are infected with the disease. The virus grows in moist areas and therefore can be transmitted even with the use of condoms.

Symptoms of Human Papilloma Virus (HPV)

Symptoms	*Symptoms*
Males	**Females**
Early Stages	*Early Stages*
Pinkish to grayish warts on the genitalia	Pinkish to grayish warts on the vulva
Difficulty in urinating	Difficulty in urinating
Later Stages	*Later Stages*
Cancer of the penis	Cancer of the cervix

Treatment

Many forms of the human papilloma virus are first treated by trichloracetic acid. If the acid treatment is not successful, warts can be removed surgically, but may reappear at any time. There is no cure.

Sexual freedom sounds great, but remember, "All Satan's apples have worms."

The Scriptures teach us two important truths: (1) that there are consequences of sin (Romans 6:23a); and (2) that because of Jesus Christ sin does not have the final word (Romans 6:23b). These truths are beautifully highlighted in the life of Peter. After the resurrection, Simon Peter had a conversation with Jesus that went like this:

"Simon, son of John, do you truly love Me more than these?"

"Yes, Lord," he said, "You know that I love You."

Jesus said, "Feed My lambs."

Again Jesus said, "Simon son of John, do you truly love Me?"

He answered, "Yes, Lord, You know that I love You."

Jesus said, "Take care of My sheep."

The third time He said to him, "Simon son of John, do you love me?"

Peter was hurt because Jesus asked him the third time, "Do you love Me?" He said, "Lord, You know all things; You know that I love You."

Jesus said, "Feed My sheep." (John 21:15–17)

Pelvic Inflammatory Disease (PID)

- There are over a million cases of PID reported each year.
- Some PID infections can be life-threatening.
- Some IUDs have been known to cause PID.

One of the most common serious diseases responsible for sterility is PID, Pelvic Inflammatory Disease. It is a genital infection usually caused by either gonorrhea or chlamydia that spreads into a woman's reproductive organs, such as the uterus, ovaries, and fallopian tubes. This can result in sterility, great pain, or an ectopic pregnancy.

Symptoms of Pelvic Inflammatory Disease (PID)

Symptoms   Fever

Nausea

Pain during intercourse

Pain in the lower abdomen

Spotting or heavy clotting during menstruation

Pain during urination

Unusual vaginal discharge

Treatment

Treatment includes bed rest and antibiotics. Sexual activity must also cease until treatment is complete. If any of the reproductive organs have scar tissue or other damage, surgery may be required.

Syphilis

- Lesions caused by syphilis greatly increase the chances of HIV infections.
- Approximately 125,000 new cases of syphilis are reported each year in the United States.
- Up to 30 percent of people with untreated syphilis report serious damage to their major organs (i.e., heart, brain).

Syphilis is an STD caused by a bacteria. Some biblical scholars believe that some of the references to leprosy in the Bible may have actually been references to those suffering from syphilis. The skin rash and spotting that often accompany syphilis made the sick look like they had leprosy.

It is mandatory in some states for couples to take blood tests before they get married to determine if either partner has syphilis. Now, because of cohabitation, many states no longer require blood tests. This means that there may be many cases of syphilis that go unreported and undetected.

Symptoms of Syphilis

Symptoms

First Stage   Cankerous, reddish sores at the spot where the
                 bacteria entered the body

Second Stage   Headaches
                 Enlargement of lymph nodes
                 Fatigue
                 Skin rash
                 Loss of appetite

Third Stage   *Condyloma lata* (raised growths that often ulcerate
                 and secrete fluid)
                 Serious damage to the nervous system
                 Serious damage to vital organs (i.e., heart, brain)

Treatment

Since syphilis is a bacterial infection, it is almost 100 percent curable with proper treatment. Over the years, the best treatment for syphilis has been penicillin. Other drugs such as tetracycline can also be used when someone is allergic to penicillin.

Other STD Infections

There are still many other STDs than the ones described above. Though they may not be deadly, such as HIV/AIDS, they are, nevertheless, bothersome and can cause serious health problems. All STDs make it even more apparent why abstinence should be practiced.

Trichomoniasis is also known as "trich." It is a common vaginal infection. Many with the disease have few symptoms. When symptoms do appear in women, they may include an unpleasant-smelling discharge from the vagina, a swelling of the groin area, and frequent urination. Men often have few symptoms but, nevertheless, carry the STD. It is effectively treated with antibiotics.

Urinary Tract Infection, or UTI, is caused by a bacterium. The bacteria usually come from the rectum to either the penis or the vagina. From there it is spread to the urethra and bladder areas and can be transmitted by sexual intercourse as well as by outercourse. The symptoms may include infection of the bladder, causing frequent and painful urination. The person may also have a fever and pain in the lower abdominal area. Most of the time urinary tract infection can be treated with antibiotics.

Chancroid is no longer as common as it once was because of the use of condoms. Chancroid can increase the chances of a person getting HIV. It is caused by bacteria called Haemophylus ducreyi. Symptoms may begin with a small pimple on the genitals. If untreated, the pimple may become ulcerated. Other symptoms might include a swelling of the lymph glands as well as a fever. Chancroid can be treated with antibiotics.

Cytomegalovirus (CMV) is an STD as well as a disease that can be passed through blood transfusion, shared needles, pregnancy, childbirth, and breast-feeding. A newborn infant can be severely affected if the mother is infected. Each year several thousand babies suffer hearing loss and are born mentally retarded because of CMV. Symptoms include fatigue, causing some to have mononucleosis. There may be a fever as well as general irritations of the digestive tract, causing diarrhea. There is no known treatment for CMV. Some intravenous drugs have proven to help curtail the disease at times.

A Final Reminder

There is only one way to have healthy, safe sex—by living according to God's standards. His standards have been already laid out for us in the first chapter of this book. Every STD is a result of sin, but not always as a result of an individual's own doing. Babies are being born with disease because of the sins of their parents. Some people are suffering from HIV/AIDS due to blood transfusions. Still other people have, in the heat of passion, taken a risk—a risk that they now regret.

Whatever the situation, the great physician God comes to heal, first by bestowing upon us the expectant forgiveness for the times we have failed and, second, by giving us physicians, drugs, and vaccines that continue to heal and treat many STDs.

No healing will ever be complete here on earth, since we live in a sinful world. However, our assurance is that we will have total healing someday in heaven: "He will wipe every tear from their eyes. There will be no more death or mourning or crying or pain, for the old order to things has passed away" (Revelation 21:4). We look forward to the day!

CHAPTER 10 Sexual Addictions

We know that the whole creation has been
groaning as in the pains of childbirth right up
to the present time. (Romans 8:22)

With sin, the God-given gift of sexuality became misunderstood and misused. Though society often judges the rightness or wrongness of sexual behavior on the basis of the cultural and social belief systems of a particular day and time, the Christian judges behavior on the basis of God's Word, a never-changing guide. For example, St. Paul reminds us that "love is kind" (1 Corinthians 13:4); therefore, any sexual activity that involves coercion or victimizes a person is seen as contrary to God's intended use of the gift. We are reminded that one of the gifts of the Holy Spirit is that of "self-control" (Galatians 5:23). When sexual behavior is so compulsive—so driven—that one no longer has self-control, it is wrong.

A Misdirected Drive

The drive for sex is as God-given as is the drive to satisfy one's hunger. Because of sin, however, both drives can be misdirected. Sex for some can become a drive that is rooted in more than just the biological need to have closeness or sexual release or to reproduce. It can become compulsive. This addiction is as serious as the addictions to alcohol and drugs. One reason for sexual addiction, similar to other addictions, is a cycle of negative feelings that are deep-rooted and can be traced back to early childhood.

Characteristics of Addictive Sex

1. It is often done in secret.
2. It often evokes feelings of guilt.
3. It is often done with little or no regard for the feelings and needs of others.
4. It is often done when a person wants to avoid pain or some other problem.
5. It is often devoid of relationship and intimacy.
6. It often victimizes by degrading, dehumanizing, or making an object of another person.

Nymphomania

Women who experience excessive sexual desire are called *nymphomaniacs*. The term comes from Greek mythology, where nymphs were female nature spirits, inhabiting and animistically representing features of nature. Nymphets were young girls who were sexually desirable, and girls who were overly sexual were called *nymphomaniacs*. The same term is used to describe someone today whose desire for sex is so great that she is unable to control her behavior even though it may mean serious consequences. The compulsion is so intense that no matter how loving and tender a nymphomaniac's partner may be, no matter how many orgasms she might experience, she still desires more.

Satyriasis

Satyriasis is a term used to describe a man who has an excessive sexual desire. In Greek mythology, a satyr was a anthropomorphic god or demon with pointed ears, legs, and short horns. These creatures were lecherous and afflicted with "satyriasis," the inability to control their sexual desires.

We do not generally hear the term *satyriasis* as much as *nymphomania*. The disparity comes from what society perceives is normal sexually for men as opposed to what is normal for females. Men who have a compulsive appetite for sex are seen as more "normal" than women who do. Such thinking stems from the traditional view that males are expected to be aggressive sexually, whereas women are to be more submissive. The truth of the matter is, both addictions are equally harmful. The incidence of occurrence is about equal in both sexes with both being equally treatable with therapy.

Just because a male or female has a high sexual drive does not mean that the person has a sexual addiction. For example, a husband may feel sexually satisfied with coitus twice a week. The wife may desire it four to five times a week. Because he has been taught to believe that men desire sex more than women, he finds himself thinking her appetite to be "abnormal," even laughing in the locker room with the other guys, telling them he's married to a "nymphomaniac."

Someone is not abnormal simply because he or she differs from others in the strength of the sex drive. When one infrequently or never has sex, it is called *hypophilia*. When one has sex more often than most people, it is called *hyperphilia*. In contrast to these "normal" ranges of sexual desire, nymphomania and satyriasis are exaggerated desires where the desire overshadows all other activities.

A 12-step program similar to the ones used to treat alcoholism and drug addiction has also proven to be successful in treating nymphomania and satyriasis. Participants in the program must acknowledge that they themselves cannot break free of this addiction and that they need a "higher power." Christians recognize that this help comes from the Triune God.

Sexual Paraphilias

Paraphiliacs are people who are sexually attracted to paraphilia, i.e., objects or situations that are not considered normal objects of sexual attraction. The American Psychiatric Association's *Diagnostic and Statistical Manual of Mental Disorders* lists a wide range of paraphilias. Many psychiatrists, psychologists, and counselors say that the rightness or wrongness of paraphilias must be determined by the culture in which they occur. Christians would say they must be judged on the basis of God's Word. Any sexual behavior that hinders a person from truly loving another person with affection and respect is problematic.

Voyeurism

Voyeurism is sexual gratification from looking at others who are engaged in a sexual act or who are nude. A voyeur will often go out of his way to "peep" at others, through people's windows or at public rest rooms. Such a person has been referred to as a "Peeping Tom." Studies have shown that voyeurs, though they are invading a person's privacy, usually do not interact physically with their victims.

Experts tell us that there is a certain amount of voyeurism in everyone. This may especially be true in our culture, where there is a great emphasis on body fitness and obsession over size of genitalia. People want to know how they compare. Thus, such "normal" voyeurism does not have sexual gratification as its major interest.

God's Word speaks clearly against voyeurism. In His Sermon on the Mountain, Jesus said, "You have heard that it was said, 'Do not commit adultery.' But I tell you that anyone who looks at a woman lustfully has already committed adultery with her in his heart" (Matthew 5:27–28). A voyeur seeks sexual gratification by looking at another person "lustfully."

Exhibitionism

Exhibitionism is the act of exposing one's genitals to someone else for the sake of receiving sexual gratification. Some studies have shown that exhibitionism stems from feelings of inadequacy. In trying to cover up feelings of inferiority about his maleness, a man will expose his penis in an attempt to prove his masculinity.

Just as in voyeurism, there may be a certain amount of exhibitionism in people today as they dress for a day at the beach or a night out on the town. Bikinis are popular for men and women. Nude beaches are becoming more and more popular in the United States. Despite the dangers of breast implants, thousands of women are receiving them every year. Men are known to pad their genital areas. Women pad their bras. Though these things may be a subtle form of exhibitionism, they do not meet the true definition if no sexual gratification is received.

Women who encounter exhibitionists find the experience to be emotionally troubling and distressing. Exhibitionism is a form of exploitation and is rightfully considered a crime.

Pedophilia

The pedophile uses a child as his object of sexual gratification. It usually involves the fondling of the child's genitals. When a female child is the object, it often includes vaginal penetration. The pedophile may also seduce the child into fondling his own sex organ and/or convince the child to engage in oral-genital sex.

Studies show that most pedophiles are personally known by their victims, and, because of this, their inappropriate activity may continue long before it is revealed to others. These same studies show that pedophiles do severe and often irreparable damage emotionally and physically to their victims. Though there have been reported cases of women engaging in this crime, most of the offenders are men. Recently pedophiles have been using the Internet to attract their victims. Often they search for boys who seem lonely and express a fear of not belonging.

The North American Man-Boy Love Association (NAMBLA) is an organization that advocates the sexual rights of children and youth. Because "sex is good," they say it "should not be denied to children any more than they are denied nourishment, education, and the freedom to explore the world around them." They feel "no one has any right to interfere with two people's right to any mutually consensual relationship."[1]

Sadomasochism

Bondage, also known as S & M, or Sadomasochism, is the application of pain or humiliation for the sake of sexual gratification. One person in the relationship has power over the other. Some bondage is known as "light bondage": One of the partner's arms and feet are tied while the other partner tickles, teases, kisses, and makes love to him or her. "Heavy bondage" is much more intense than simply tying a partner's arms or legs. It usually involves the use of chains, whips, and other devices to inflict pain. For those in heavy bondage, pain is invigorating and sexual. There are bondage clubs in most major cities in the United States that cater to S & M (e.g., "Chicago Hellfire Club," "Leather and Lace in L.A.").

Most people wonder why some adults enjoy being spanked or whipped, or enjoy spanking or whipping others. Some experts believe that it has to do with humiliation and shame the participants experienced as a child and that, by sexualizing it, the past humiliation and shame becomes more bearable. Whatever the deep psychological reasons for such sexual behavior, one's participation in S & M contradicts God's words to us in Holy Scripture: "Do you not know that your body is a temple of the Holy Spirit, who is in you, whom you have received from God? You are not your own; you were bought at a price. Therefore honor God with your body" (1 Corinthians 6:19–20). Sadomasochism is a sign of more than physical bondage; it denotes spiritual bondage as well.

Other Paraphilias

Though the above-mentioned paraphilias are the ones most heard about, there are a myriad of others as well: people become sexually aroused from the use of a particular prop (e.g., underwear), body part (e.g., feet) or given situation (e.g., shoplifting). Because they are less common, often these paraphilias are mislabeled and misunderstood, thus not always treated as they should be.

Less Common Paraphilias

Paraphilia	Description
Biastophilia	Arousal comes from sexually attacking someone unexpectedly
Frotteurism	Arousal comes from anonymously pressing or rubbing one's genitals against another, usually in a public, crowded place.
Necrophilia	Arousal comes from sex with a dead person
Pictophilia	Arousal comes from viewing pornography
Transvestophilia	Arousal comes from wearing clothing, such as underwear, of the opposite sex
Asphyxophilia	Arousal comes from strangulation

Kleptophilia	Arousal comes from stealing things
Saliromania	Arousal comes from damaging or soiling the body or clothing of a woman
Klismaphilia	Arousal comes from taking enemas
Pyromania	Arousal comes from setting fires
Homocidophilia	Arousal comes from thinking about murdering one's partner
Acrotomophilia	Arousal comes from imagining one is an amputee
Mysophilia	Arousal comes from soiled underwear
Narratophilia	Arousal comes from erotic narratives

At times the word *fetishism* and *paraphilia* are used interchangeably in describing the sexual attraction that comes from a particular object, substance, or part of the body. As the fetishist looks at these objects (even fondling them at times) or situations, he often masturbates. Objects can include everything from hats to underwear. Though most men find looking at women's breasts stimulating, fetishism is an intensification of the normal attraction. A fetishist may be someone who cannot perform sexually without his or her partner talking "dirty" during the sexual act. A fetishist may be someone who finds sexual satisfaction in piercing his or her genitalia. Fetishism can include a practice called "handballing" or "vaginal fisting," in which the woman receives pleasure from having her partner jam his or her fist into the vagina.

The War Within

Sexual addictions are not new to our culture or our day and age. the Bible tells us "there is nothing new under the sun" (Ecclesiastes 1:9). Take the story of David. Here was a man of God who showed the world what it was like to trust God explicitly as he took on the Philistine giant and defeated him. But he was also the one who was unable to defeat within himself the desire to commit adultery with Bathsheba.

Most sexual addictions cannot be defeated by one's own will power. It can only be done with God's help and the counsel of people God surrounds us with in the way of Christian therapists and counselors, friends and pastors. Remember, Christ defeated Satan and sin with His life, death, and resurrection. He can help us defeat addiction as well.

For our struggle is not against flesh and blood, but against the rulers, against the authorities, against the powers of this dark world and against the spiritual forces of evil in the heavenly realms. Therefore put on the full armor of God. (Ephesians 6:12–13)

"Sexual addiction is a fantasy the addicted create to cope with inescapable loneliness. The photographers and editors of pornographic magazines know how to sustain the illusion. The hooker knows how to dress and talk to create the illusion. The voice on the other end of the 900 number knows what to say. They know the techniques to tap into addicts' desires and needs. But the payoff is just money. 'I know a prostitute doesn't really love or accept me,' a patient said to me during a counseling session, 'but she pretends she does and I enjoy the illusion. I really know that to a hooker there are only two kinds of men: clean and unclean. Money is really the bottom line.' Another patient said, 'If I can hook him with sex, I'll have the relationship I need!' She then added, 'Somewhere there's a man who will want sex and love me—there's just gotta be!'

"The fantasies of a sex addict are feeble attempts to gain what only God is capable of giving, which we will experience partially on earth and fully in heaven."[2]

CHAPTER 11	**Ways of Feeding the Sexual Appetite**

The purposes of a man's heart are deep waters. (Proverbs 20:5)

The heart is deceitful above all things and beyond cure. (Jeremiah 17:9)

One day my mother found my *Penthouse* and *Playboy* magazines that I had hidden back in my closet. She was so angry she made me go see our pastor. He quoted passage after passage from Scripture about the sinfulness of such magazines. I told him and my mom I'd never look at them again. I don't. Now I have the Internet. I don't need the magazines anymore. Now I just surf the porno sites. I see all of what I saw in the magazines and even more—and I never worry about my mom finding the stuff. I just turn off my computer and the stuff's gone ... at least until tomorrow, when I go surfing for it again and find that and even more." —a 15-year-old teenager

Pornography

The word *pornography* comes from two Greek words: *porne*, "a harlot," and *graphein*, "to write." The word literally means "the writing of a harlot." Pornography was a major problem in Corinth when Paul wrote his first letter to the Christians in that city. It was not only tolerated but was very much a part of the worship in the temple of Aphrodite at Corinth. Today, with the advancement of technology, pornography can be experienced by all five of the senses. It can be viewed in the privacy of our living rooms or as one is speeding down a freeway and glances over to see a huge billboard advertising the latest cologne. Today the selling of pornography is one of the biggest money makers on the Internet.

Used interchangeably with the word *pornography* is the word *obscenity*. *Obscenity* refers to utterances, gestures, and the like that are offensive to public taste and morals—anything that "appeals to prurient interests." The secular world as well as the church has debated for years over what is considered pornographic and obscene.

Erotica is often thought of as different from pornography in that it presents nudity or sexual activity in an artistic way. It displays its subjects with respect and affection as compared to pornography, which shows subjects in a degrading way, as objects more than as people, often using violence in its depiction. However, when any artist goes beyond the limits of what is decent and acceptable spiritually and morally, even if it's called "erotic art," it should rightfully be censured by Christians.

A Confession of a Killer

Serial killer Ted Bundy had the following to say just before he was executed for the murder of 12-year-old Kimberly Leach:

"This is the message I want to get across: As a young boy, and I mean a boy of 12 or 13, I encountered ... in the local grocery store and in the local drug store, the soft-core pornography that people call "soft core". ... I tell you that I am not blaming pornography. I am not saying that it caused me to go out and do certain things. And I take full responsibility for whatever I've done. ... That's not the question here. The question and the issue is how this kind of literature contributed and helped mold and shape these kinds of violent behavior ... In the beginning it fuels this kind of thought process. Then, at a certain time it's instrumental—I would say crystallizing, making it into something which is almost like a separate entity inside... . Once you've become addicted to pornography—and this is a kind of addiction like other kinds of addiction— I would keep looking for more potent, more explicit, more graphic kinds of material. ... You begin to wonder if maybe actually doing it will give you that which is beyond just reading about it or looking at it. ... I've lived in prison for a long time now and I've met a lot of men who are motivated to commit violence just like me. And without exception, every one of them was deeply involved in pornography—without question, without exception, deeply influenced and consumed by an addiction to pornography.... The FBI's own study on serial homicide shows that the most common interest among serial killers is pornography."[1]

As in all addictions, the addiction to pornography doesn't stand still. There is always the desire for more excitement. The addiction demands to see more and experience more. It wants the next level of titillation. James writes: "Then, after desire has conceived, it gives birth to sin; and sin, when it is full-grown, gives birth to death" (James 1:15). The pornographers know that if they are going to stay in business they have to keep satisfying their reader's or viewer's sexual appetite or they will lose them to another vendor. For example, a leading pornographic men's magazine found its circulation declining over the years because of the proliferation of pornography on the Internet and more graphic depictions of sexuality in competitive magazines. An editorial decision was made to introduce more graphic and sexual pictures into their magazine.

"Pornographic magazines are the fifth most discarded item in hotels."[2]

"I have all the money I need now and I'm not really motivated by it anymore. The most important contribution I could make would be an end to the obscenity laws."[3]

Studies have repeatedly shown a direct correlation between the availability of pornography with abusive sexual activity such as rape. A study of Oklahoma County, Oklahoma, "showed that as the number of pornography outlets were closed, the number of rapes went down." During a five-year period where there was a strict enforcement of laws against obscenity and pornography the rape rate dropped more than 26 percent.[4]

"Pornography is the theory, and rape is the practice."[5]

Videos

Hard-core videos are now available in almost every city and community, in almost every local liquor store, in almost every video store. These videos cater to almost every conceivable predilection. There are bondage videos, gay videos, straight he/she videos, sadomasochistic videos, etc. Though men are the largest consumers of these videos, more and more women are viewing them. One survey indicates that Americans are spending over $3.9 billion dollars a year renting or buying adult videos.

"Adult" Videos

A survey of 19,000 video store retailers reported the following statistics on the rental of pornographic videos:

1996—$3.8 billion

1995—$3.1 billion

1994—$2.5 billion

Music

One of the most effective communication vehicles is music—everything from rap to heavy metal, country western to soft rock, classical to jazz. Studies show that the average teenager will spend as much time listening to rock music as he or she spends in the classroom each year. A lead article in *Time* magazine asked the question, "Are Music and Movies Killing America's Soul?"[6] Though the answer varied depending on who was being asked the question, a poll indicated that 62 percent wanted more restrictions on the lyrics of popular music.

The reason for such thinking is that many of the kids' CD collections contain words such not even permitted on TV. Some songs encourage sex without condoms. One popular rap song and video show a salesgirl physically abused by a gang of sadistic bikers. Still another shows the lead singer having sex with a woman as he's squeezing her head in a vice-like grip. A snake crawls between them.

In analyzing the content of the videos that appeal so powerfully to ... adolescents, and featured round-the-clock on MTV, the national

Coalition on Television violence found that 68 percent of them contained at least one of the following elements: explicit violence, suggestions of violence, sexually suggestive themes, profanity, smoking, and/or alcohol consumption."[7]

"Let us throw off everything that hinders and the sin that so easily entangles."
(Hebrews 12:1)

Television

Almost every home has one or more televisions. A survey of children in grades 3 through 12 found that they watch an average of 21 hours of television per week. Fifty-four percent of four- to six-year-olds said they would rather watch television than spend time with their fathers. Up to 70 percent of all teenagers have televisions in their bedrooms. Surveys have shown that when teenagers watch television alone they watch different programs than when they're sitting in the same room with their parents, many times programs filled with sex and violence. Monique Ward, a post-doctoral student at the University of California at Los Angeles, analyzed the sexual content in the 1992–93 prime-time shows that were most watched by young people 2 to 12 and 12 to 17. "On average, 29 percent of all interactions involved sex talk of some kind." Ward also found that sex is often depicted as an "exciting amusement for people of all ages."[8] Another survey found that 88 percent of all sexual relationships shown on television were between unmarried people.

David Walsh, in his book *Selling Out America's Children*, suggests that we have become a society where the only operative question is "Will it make money?"

As a society, we Americans of the late twentieth century are sacrificing our children at the altar of financial gain. We are selling out America's children for money. Although we are often not consciously aware of it, maximizing profit is more important to us than asking ourselves whether or not something is beneficial or harmful to our children.[9]

What Should Parents Do?

Parents should not just sit and wait for television to get better, to support moral values. The networks will only stop producing what they are when the public says "enough is enough." Public opinion led Calvin Klein to pull its controversial ads of children posing in underwear in seductive poses. Advertisers care what the public thinks, especially when it comes to their profits. More importantly, if parents really want to eliminate inappropriate television, they themselves need to turn off the television when it advocates values contrary to what they expound. As someone said, "Children won't grow up until their parents do."

A Study of TV's "Family Hour"—8 to 9 P.M. Eastern Time

75 percent of family-hour shows contain sexual behavior or verbal references to sex.

There is an average of 8.5 incidents of sexual behavior in each hour of programming.

In comparison to 1976, where 26 percent of family-hour programs contained sexual behavior, in 1996, 61 percent did so.

Only 6 percent showed any risk or responsibility to the sexual activity being shown or discussed.[10]

Telephone Sex

Telephone sex is when someone calls a number for the explicit purpose of having someone talk to him or her in a sexually provocative way. Pornographic magazines are filled with advertisements luring its readers into talk about sex: "Talk Live with REAL HUNKS, 1-800-BIG-HUNK"; "Fetish Connection on the Phone! Call 1-800-555-3425," "Intimate Phone Sex—1-800-INT-MATE." Sometimes the caller masturbates as the man or woman on the line talks dirty. Telephone sex is a booming business because it allows men and women to retain their anonymity while experiencing sexual gratification. One survey indicates that Americans are spending close to $1 billion annually on telephone sex.

Closely connected is something called *telephone scatologia*—obscene telephone calls. The caller is often driven by feelings of inadequacy and inferiority. The calls are frightening, to say the least, but studies show that the callers seldom follow up with any physical contact with the one being called.

Radio

The radio is one of the most-used vehicles for communication. Just as talk/interview shows have become a mainstay for the television industry, so such shows featuring different personalities have become popular on the radio. One of the more popular radio personalities, Howard Stern, almost daily talks about sexuality in the crudest of ways. His conversations are often about such subjects as bestiality and prostitution. It is not uncommon for him to have female guests undress in the studios in front of himself and Robin, his co-host, and perform lesbian sex as the show is being broadcast.

Howard Stern and other radio personalities continue to push free speech to the limits without taking any responsibility for who might be listening and the effects it might be having on them. The huge success of the show has attracted a whole host of "wannabe shock jocks" who duplicate Stern's crude sexual content. Though the FCC has repeatedly sued Infinity Broadcasting, owner of *The Howard Stern Show*, for indecency, the fines have been minimal in comparison to the large amounts of money earned due to the popularity of the show.

Cybersex

Ours is called the "Age of Information," due in large part to computers. By connecting computer networks, we now have what we call the "Internet." People from all over the world can talk to one another about any imaginable subject. They can buy and sell using the Internet. They can teach and learn through the Internet. The Internet has also opened up new avenues to sex-oriented services and communications. With a few clicks of the mouse, one can enter into hundreds of "chat rooms," meeting and talking with almost any imaginable group of people:

Hairy Chest M4M
I love older women
LONG ISLAND DUNGEON
BiCuriousMarriedMen
black lesbians

Using any of the on-line services such as America OnLine, CompuServe, or Prodigy, anyone can wander into sexually explicit chat rooms. Literally millions of kids go on-line every year and, as they explore, they find it easy to pull up sexually explicit pictures in a matter of minutes. More and more adults are engaged in what is called *cybersex*, meaning they engage in sex with one another via the Internet. Two people chat with one another and as they do, each person masturbates, freeing themselves of any personal face-to-face contact as well as any obligations. In essence, it enables the most prudish person to pursue secret desires from behind a facade.

One man said, "It's my opportunity to share my deepest, darkest fantasies with someone who fantasizes with me. My wife would think I'm sick if I told her these things." Cyberspace provides a way to uncover and exploit our secrets without the danger of getting caught. Marriages are perhaps as affected as any institution by this new technology.

The dangers of living in a fantasy world are obvious. Psychologists warn us against getting wrapped up in a "reality" that is not real. Some suggest that the addiction to fantasize sex is similar to any other addiction: It literally alters a person's mood and demeanor to the point where he or she can't distinguish between what is real and what is unreal. Some would suggest that the Internet provides an opportunity for people to cheat without really cheating. It is clear from Scripture that "cheating" begins in the heart: "There are six things the LORD hates … a heart that devises wicked schemes" (Proverbs 6:16, 18).

In June of 1997, the Supreme Court struck down the Communications Decency Act, which made it a crime to send or display indecent or obscene material over the Internet where it could be seen by children. The justices said that the law was too broad because it would prevent adults from viewing indecent and obscene material if they so desired. Justice John Paul Stevens, writing for the majority, stated that it was highly unlikely that children would just accidentally happen upon obscene material on the Internet.

One of the areas of concern by the government has been the recent rash of children who have been lured into relationships with pedophiles through the Internet. Letting children explore unsupervised on the Internet is dangerous, to say the least. Parental supervision is essential. There are software programs that can help parents set up roadblocks to certain sites and chat rooms.

A free brochure entitled "Child Safety on the Information Highway" can be ordered from the National Center for Missing and Exploited Children and Interactive Services Association (1-800-843-5678). It provides tips that help you talk to your child about On-Line safety.

Estimated Web shopping revenues by sector-industry

Computer products	27.0 percent
Travel	24.3 percent
Adult entertainment	9.9 percent
Apparel	8.9 percent
Gifts-flowers	8.7 percent
Food/drink	7.5 percent
General entertainment	6.5 percent
Other	7.2 percent
Total	$518 million[11]

A Twelve-Step Program

There are 12-step group recovery programs available for sexually addicted people just as there are Alcoholic Anonymous and Overeaters Anonymous groups. The one requirement for participation is a desire to end one's addiction. Here is a list of a few of the groups available:

SAA (Sex Addicts Anonymous)
P.O. Box 3038
Minneapolis, MN 55403
(612-871-1520)

SCA (Sexual Compulsives Anonymous)
P.O. Box 1585
Old Chelsea Station
New York, NY 10113
(800-977-4325)

SA (Sexaholics Anonymous)
P.O. Box 300
Simi Valley, CA 93062
(805-581-3343)

Healing Is Available

Many aspects of our culture emphasize immediate gratification of the flesh—meeting our needs before considering the needs of others. Though there are many reasons for sexual addiction and dangerous sexual behavior, the root cause is always sin.

Satan, the Prince of Darkness, is no fool. He engulfs the world with lurid literature, making it so exciting that normalcy seems pale in comparison. He gets columnists to say that rappers who sing about killing cops and raping women are simply misunderstood. His tactic is working and is gradually making his audiences desensitized to violence and sexual misconduct, making them desirous of more. He has even convinced the so-called experts, the psychologists and therapists, to redefine some sexual misconduct, making it simply an alternative and unique way of enjoying one's sexuality.

Through the power of God and His abiding love and mercy, there is help. It begins with brokenness, repentance, and a deep, sincere, grasping for God's help. It's the cry of St. Paul and all sinners: "What a wretched man I am! Who will rescue me from this body of death? Thanks be to God—through Jesus Christ our Lord!" (Romans 7:24–25).

CHAPTER 12 — Sexual Problems

I slept but my heart was awake.
  Listen! My lover is knocking:
"Open to me, my sister, my darling,
  my dove, my flawless one.
My head is drenched with dew,
  my hair with the dampness of the night."
I have taken off my robe—
  must I put it on again?
I have washed my feet—
  must I soil them again?
My lover thrust his hand through the latch-opening;
  my heart began to pound for him.
I arose to open for my lover,
  and my hands dripped with myrrh,
my fingers with flowing myrrh,
  on the handles of the lock.
I opened for my lover,
  but my lover had left; he was gone.
My heart sank at his departure.
I looked for him but did not find him.
  I called him but he did not answer. (Song of Songs 5:2–6)

We live in a world where, from television to the Internet, the most frequently used word is *sex*. Few things about it seem off limits. In 1972, the program *Maude* featured the lead character choosing abortion as her method of birth control. In 1989, a program called *thirtysomething* featured two naked, gay men lying in bed together, chatting. Dan Quayle was literally destroyed politically by the media over a negative comment he made about a 1991 episode of *Murphy Brown* where the leading character decided to become a single mother. A few years later, the program *Seinfeld* had its audience laughing about everything from masturbation to the size of an actor's genitalia. Then there was the controversial episode of *Ellen* in 1997, which featured the lead character coming out of the closet, announcing she was gay.

All the joking and laughter about masturbation, about whether or not one needs a husband to raise a child, has not only, too often, presented a skewed and distorted picture of these subjects, but has also driven people further "into the closet" in divulging their own personal sexual problems. The picture presented seems to be that everyone—from the heterosexual to the homosexual—is sexually enjoying their maleness and femaleness. Though they may have to deal with some of the moral issues as abortion and gayness, they are, nevertheless, enjoying sex.

Certainly, according to the media, anyone who is anybody doesn't have a problem with impotence! or premature ejaculation! or trouble reaching an orgasm! Our leaders, our heroes, are all having great sex! The hero of many, assassinated President John F. Kennedy, reportedly had to deal with only one problem—finding the time and the place to see his many secret lady friends. One accuser let the courts and the news media know that she could identify certain unusual characteristics of a president's penis because he had asked her to perform oral sex on him. Even a leading television evangelist was caught propositioning a prostitute. A star basketball player announced he had AIDS, because, as he said, he had "tried to accommodate as many women as he could."

Once again, the message seems to be that everyone, from the president of the United States to one's favorite television evangelist, though perhaps not being as moral as they ought to be, is performing well in the bedroom. All of these things only make anyone who might be experiencing any sexual problems go even more underground than before!

There was a grand celebration in a local retirement home for an elderly couple who had been married for 65 years. The local newspaper sent a reporter to ask the couple some questions.

"Do you have any children?" the reported asked.

"Not yet!" the man said, as he looked at his wife and winked.

Think about what the very word *impotence* conveys—failure, lack of manhood. What about the word *frigid?* The word suggests that the woman is cold and insensitive. Who would want to tell a friend at the gym that he's got some problems with "his manhood," with "impotence?"

Despite all the talk about sex and the glamorization of it, studies say that 10 to 20 percent of all men and women report incidences of sexual dysfunction. It is rightfully assumed that, because of the personal nature of a sexual dysfunction, many people are simply too uncomfortable talking about it, and so the rate of incidence may be higher than reported. The more common dysfunctions include the following:

For Men

• Premature Ejaculation

• Impotence

For Women

• Vaginismus and Dyspareunia

• Failure to reach orgasm

Sexual Dysfunctions of Men

Premature Ejaculation

In premature ejaculation, ejaculation occurs before a man wants it to occur. A common problem: The husband ejaculates before his wife reaches an orgasm.

There are many degrees of premature ejaculation. It can range from someone who needs only to see an attractive woman and ejaculates in his pants to a person who climaxes shortly after he inserts his penis into the woman's vagina. The more he thinks about the problem and worries about it, the more he loses his ability to really give himself totally to sexual pleasure. He may feel so inadequate as a lover that he simply withdraws physically and emotionally from his spouse.

A number of techniques can help. Condoms cut down on penile sensitivity and allow the man to hold off ejaculating. Other methods include masturbation before sexual intercourse, using different positions in lovemaking, and thinking about something totally unrelated to the sexual act itself.

Since the problem is not just the "man's problem," but instead is the "couple's problem," both need to work on it. They may, for example, try "the Squeeze," a technique developed by sex therapists. Upon sensing that he is close to ejaculation, the husband or his wife squeezes or pinches the penis for several seconds where the glans joins the shaft. This decreases the flow of blood, causing the man to lose part of his erection. It can be repeated as often as needed in order to help control ejaculation.

Other Sensual Areas on the Male Anatomy

A woman can help delay her husband's orgasm and perhaps help herself to reach orgasm simultaneously, by touching other sensitive areas on her lover other than his penis. Some of these areas include his nipples, scrotum, buttocks, and perineum (the area between the anus and genitalia).

Impotence

Impotence, the opposite problem to that of premature ejaculation, is difficulty in getting or maintaining an erection. Contrary to popular belief, the problem is not unique to older men. Even the newly married young man can experience an embarrassing moment when he cannot get or maintain an erection. Many factors can contribute to this problem: alcohol, stress, illness, medication.

> Estimations are that 30 million men in
> the United States suffer from impotence.

Sometimes men suffer from impotence as a result of reduced blood supply to the penis. This may be brought about by high blood pressure or some heart disease. It may be caused by the medicine that is taken to lower one's blood pressure. Whatever the reason, men do not have to live with impotence. There are many treatments available. If, for example, medication seems to be affecting a man's ability to maintain an erection, he should talk to his doctor about changing medication.

One of the easiest cures to impotence has been to simply change one's sexual habits. An erection is nothing more than blood flowing into a man's penis. If he is too tired, this may not happen as easily as it once did. The best time for sexual pleasure might be in the morning, just after waking up, when one is feeling refreshed and relaxed. It is also true that early in the morning the male's sex hormone, testosterone, is at its highest level.

Other techniques and helpful interventions are available when a change in a man's lifestyle doesn't seem to help. These interventions range from having a penile implant to injecting into the penis vasoactive drugs. One device that doesn't require surgery or any injection is a vacuum-constriction device—a vacuum pump that is placed over the penis. Air is pumped out of the device, pulling blood into the penis and causing an erection. Once an erection has been achieved, a ring is placed around the base of the penis to keep the erection.

An Erection Drug

A drug called *alprostadil* is approved by the FDA to help produce an erection. It is self-injected into the base of the penis and produces an erection within 5–20 minutes.

A new pill, introduced in 1998, called *Viagra* is being used successfully by thousands of men to conquer impotency. The drug works by prolonging the effects of cyclic GMP, the chemical in the penis that causes the muscles to relax and the arteries to expand.

Unfortunately, medical doctors do not always know how to treat men suffering from impotence and so they are not always the best people to talk to. The one medical professional an impotent man might want to speak to is a urologist. Urologists are trained to provide help to those who suffer with this problem. There is help available, and no man—young or old—has to live with impotence if he doesn't want to.

Other Male Sexual Dysfunctions

A less common problem for men is retarded (or delayed) ejaculation. It occurs when a man cannot ejaculate no matter how long he maintains an erection. There are many factors that can contribute to this dysfunction. One should first consult with a doctor to make sure there is nothing wrong physically. If the problem is psychological, one may need to see a therapist.

Some men suffer with *priapism*, or a permanent erection that is not only unwanted but painful. Priapism can be caused by blood being so thick that once it flows into the penis it has difficulty leaving again. One disease that causes such thickening of the blood is sickle-cell anemia. It can also be caused by overuse of the drug cocaine.

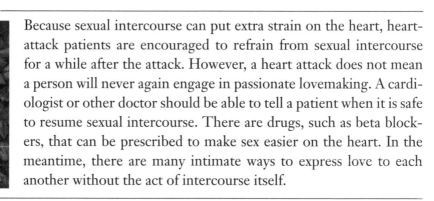

Because sexual intercourse can put extra strain on the heart, heart-attack patients are encouraged to refrain from sexual intercourse for a while after the attack. However, a heart attack does not mean a person will never again engage in passionate lovemaking. A cardiologist or other doctor should be able to tell a patient when it is safe to resume sexual intercourse. There are drugs, such as beta blockers, that can be prescribed to make sex easier on the heart. In the meantime, there are many intimate ways to express love to each another without the act of intercourse itself.

Sexual Dysfunctions of Women

Vaginismus and Dyspareunia

Vaginismus is an involuntary spasm of the muscles within the vagina that makes intercourse painful and often impossible. Though the dysfunction can be caused by a physical problem such as an abscess on the vagina, most of the time vaginismus is a psychological problem. The psychological reasons may include everything from guilt over having sex to some traumatic experience such as rape.

Vaginismus is treatable. It begins with honest and open communication between a husband and wife. It includes studying what God's Word says about the gift of sex. It means doing some home exercises (e.g., practicing contraction and relaxation of the vaginal muscles). It may take some time, patience, and work, but eventually a couple will be able to overcome this problem.

Closely related to vaginismus is a dysfunction called *dyspareunia*. Dyspareunia is painful intercourse. A number of factors can contribute to this problem, such as dryness of the vagina, tumors in the reproductive organs, STDs, and vaginal infections. Dyspareunia can also be psychologically induced by such things as guilt over sex or unresolved conflict with one's husband. If a woman does experience painful intercourse, an important first stip is to see a physician and have a thorough physical examination, especially a complete pelvic exam. If dryness of the vagina seems to be the problem, a lubrication can be recommended by a pharmacist. If it is determined that it is not a physical problem, one should consult a therapist.

Failure to Reach Orgasm

The word *orgasm* comes from the Greek word *orgasmus*, meaning "a ripening, a swelling." There are a number of related words that people use to describe an orgasm, such as *climax* and *coming*. An orgasm is a "ripening" of the sexual act itself. For women, an orgasm is a series of rhythmic contractions brought about by physical and psychological stimulation. The number and frequency of these contractions vary with individuals. When a woman has an orgasm, muscles in the uterus and the first third of the vagina contract. Because it is brought about by blood flow, some women actually report having postorgasmic contractions hours after sexual intercourse.

Men and women often base their sexual prowess on their ability not only to have orgasms themselves but also their ability to give their partners orgasms. Therefore, when a woman fails to have an orgasm, it may not only affect her but her husband. He may feel like he has failed as a lover. Estimates are that five to 20 percent of women are unable to reach orgasm.

Studies have shown that some women who are unable to have an orgasm tend to have a negative attitude about sex, perhaps even guilt over "having sex." Therefore, a woman needs to talk openly with her husband about the problem. She needs to tell him what feels good, where it feels good, and what she'd like him to do to her before, during, and after intercourse. If a husband and wife working together can't eliminate the elements blocking a sexual response, a Christian therapist should be consulted.

> "The subject of geriatric sex has been taboo for far too long and, because of this, the elderly are discriminated against."[1]

Old Age and Sex

One of the myths about making love is that it ceases after one reaches a certain age. Some actually believe that the older adult is asexual. Aging may bring about some changes in human sexual performance but it does not necessarily reduce the desire. Both sexual capacity and desire are lifelong. Sexual behavior and the act of making love is primarily a function of the brain. One important part of the brain is the *thalamus*, which literally means "bedroom" in Greek.

Sometimes, especially for the older male, the ability to have an orgasm may lessen but generally does not cease. It just may not occur every time lovemaking takes place. More physical stimulation may be needed to produce and maintain an erection. For the woman who has stopped producing natural lubrication, there are also many purchased lubricants that will help. As discussed previously in this chapter, there are many techniques and helpful interventions that are available for those who want to enjoy their gift of sexuality in the later years of life.

Though a couple may have to give up many things as they get older—employment, mobility—they do not have to give up the God-given gift of making love to one another. Surveys are telling us the majority of them don't. One survey showed that 54 percent of those between 60 and 93 years of age are sexually active.[2]

Treatment of All Sexual Problems

Treatment of sexual problems cannot be reduced to a few suggested mechanical steps, especially since, as we have seen, sex is more than what two people do physically. For the Christian, having sex is making love. It is something that is physical, emotional, and spiritual. Treating any sexual dysfunction requires more than learning specific skills to remove some of the barriers to normal sexual functioning. It requires an examination of attitude and mind-set. It means looking at the facts and not some mythical standards that have come from the producers of the most recent popular sitcom on television. It requires dealing with sin, guilt, forgiveness, and absolution. It requires honest communication over fear of failure or one's need to please.

It means knowing what God says about sex and, in seeing His affirmation of it, fully enjoying it without guilt.

Notes

Chapter 1: Sexuality? It Was God's Idea!

1. C. S. Lewis, *The Four Loves* (New York: Harcourt Brace & Company, 1960), 170.

2. Stanley J. Grenz, *Sexual Ethics: An Evangelical Perspective* (Louisville: Westminister John Knox Press, 1990), 45.

3. Elaine Storkey, *The Search for Intimacy* (Grand Rapids: Eerdmans, 1995), 5–6.

4. Clifford and Joyce Penner, *The Gift of Sex* (Waco: Word Books, 1981), 38.

5. John Barrymore as quoted in *Leo Rosten's Carnival of Wit: From Aristotle to Groucho Marx*, ed. by Leo Rosten, (New York: A Plume Book, published by the Penguin Group, 1994), 442.

6. John Gray, *Mars and Venus in the Bedroom* (New York: HarperCollins, 1995), 20.

7. Tim and Beverly LaHaye, *The Act of Marriage*, (Grand Rapids: Zondervan, 1976), 223.

8. Malcolm Bradbury as quoted in *Carnival of Wit*, 443.

9. Michael J. McManus, *Marriage Savers: How to Help Your Friends and Family Avoid Divorce*, (Grand Rapids: Zondervan, 1993), 36–37.

10. Norval D. Glenn, "Marriage Is Not a Dirty Word," *Los Angeles Times*, 16 September 1997, B-7.

11. Leon R. Yankewich, as quoted in *Cassell's Dictionary of Sex Quotations*, (London: Market House Books, 1993), 224.

12. Mike Robinson, *"Ignorance May Mean More Sex,"* *Pasadena Star News*, 15 January 1998, C-6.

Chapter 2: Gender and Sexual Orientation

1. Larry Burtoft, *Setting the Record Straight* (Colorado Springs: Focus on the Family, 1994), 8.

2. *American Family Association Journal*, 22, no. 1:8.

3. Ed Young, *Pure Sex* (Sisters, OR: Multnomah, 1997), 155.

4. Joseph Nicolosi, *Reparative Therapy of Male Homosexuality: A New Clinical Approach*, (Northvale, NJ: Jason Aronson, Inc., 1991), xvi.

5. Robert T. Michael, John H. Gagnon, Edward O. Laumann, and Gina Kolata, *Sex in America: A Definitive Survey* (New York: Little, Brown and Company, 1994), 174–75.

6. Nicolosi, *Reparative Therapy of Male Homosexuality*, 111.

7. Ibid., 127–28.

8. C. W. Scudder, *The Family in Christian Perspective* (Nashville: Broadman Press, 1962), 31–32.

Chapter 3: The Bodies We Have

1. William Masters and Virginia Johnson as quoted in *Dictionary of Sex Quotations*, 178.

2. Merrill F. Unger, *Unger's Bible Dictionary* (Chicago: Moody, 1976), 207.

3. Lennart Nilsson, *A Child Is Born* (New York: Dell, 1990), 42.

4. From a survey by Glen Wilson and David Nias, as reported by Harold Ivan Smith in *Singles Ask: Answers to Questions about Relationships and Sexual Issues* (Minneapolis: Augsburg Fortress, 1988), 42.

Chapter 4: Ways of "Making Love"

1. Graham Masterton, as quoted in *Dictionary of Sex Quotations*, 265.

2. Dr. Alex Comfort, as quoted in *Dictionary of Sex Quotations*, 268.

3. Erasmus, as quoted in *Dictionary of Sex Quotations*, Cassell, 264.

4. Kevin Leman, *Sex Begins in the Kitchen* (Ventura: Regal, 1981), 148–49.

5. Gary Smalley and John Trent, *The Blessing* (New York: Pocket Books, 1986), 46.

6. Penner, *The Gift of Sex*, 89–90.

7. Elaine Storkey, *The Search for Intimacy*, 194.

Chapter 5: Sex and the Single Person

1. Robert T. Michael, et al, *Sex in America*, 91–92.
2. Ibid., 93–94.
3. "Was It Good for Us?" *U.S. News and World Report* 122, no. 19 (19 May 1997), 47.
4. Ed Young, *Pure Sex*, 120.
5. UK government-sponsored AIDS advertisement, as quoted in *Dictionary of Sex Quotations*, 254.
6. "Was It Good for Us?" 56.
7. Robert T. Michael, et al, *Sex in America*, 158.
8. Ibid., 158–59.
9. *Singles Ask*, 131.
10. Storkey, *The Search for Intimacy* 195.
11. Leland Elliot and Cynthia Branthey, *Sex on Campus* (New York: Random House, 1997), 171–72.
12. R. O. Ogletree, "Sexual Coercion Experience and Help-Seeking Behavior of College Women," *Journal of American College Health*, vol. 41 (January 1993).

Chapter 6: Family Planning

1. "News You Can Use," *U.S. News and World Report* 122, no. 8 (3 March 1997), 66.
2. F. LaGard Smith, *When Choice Becomes God* (Eugene: Harvest House, 1990), 139–40.
3. Michael Novak, "Personally Opposed," *National Review* 49, no. 8 (5 May 1997), 47.
4. R. C. Sproul, *Abortion: A Rational Look at an Emotional Issue*, (Colorado Springs: Navpress, 1990), 53–54.
5. Scott B. Rae, *Brave New Families* (Grand Rapids: Baker, 1996), 104–8.
6. Roger and Robin Sonnenberg, *Living with Infertility*, (St. Louis: Concordia, 1994), 35–36.

Chapter 7: Reproduction

1. Martin Luther, as quoted in *Dictionary of Sex Quotations*, 222.

2. Robert G. Wells, Ken Gire, Mary C. Wells, and Judy Gire, *Miracle of Life: Devotions for Expectant Mothers* (Grand Rapids: Zondervan, 1993), introduction.

Chapter 8: Infertility Advances

1. *FDA Consumer* 31, no. 1 (January 1997), 18.

2. Rae, *Brave New Families*, 13–14.

3. Ibid., 15.

4. Ibid., 171.

5. John Klotz, *Life Choices, Who Decides? Following God's Word in Life and Death Decisions* (St. Louis: Concordia, 1991), 67–68.

6. "The New Revolution in Making Babies," *Time* (1 December 1997), 46.

Chapter 9: Sexually Transmitted Diseases

1. Spencer A. Rathus and Susan Boughn, *AIDS* (Orlando: Harcourt Brace College Publishers, 1994), 70.

Chapter 10: Sexual Addictions

1. Burtoft, *Setting the Record Straight*, 65–66.

2. Harry W. Schaumburg, *False Intimacy: A Biblical Understanding of Sexual Addiction* (Colorado Springs: NavPress, 1997), 31.

Chapter 11: Ways of Feeding the Sexual Appetite

1. Excerpted from the video *Fatal Addiction* published by *Focus on the Family*. Copyright © 1989, Gocus on the Family. All rights reserved. International copyright secured. Used by permission.

2. From Guardian, as quoted in *Dictionary of Sex Quotations*, 126.

3. Larry Flynt, as quoted by *U.S. News & World Report* 122, no. 5 (10 February 1997), 45.

4. *Pornography: Is Your Family Safe?* 15.

5. Robin Morgan, as quoted in *Dictionary of Sex Quotations*, 188.

6. "Unpopular Culture," *Time* 145, no. 24 (12 June 1995), 25–39.

7. Michael Medved, *Hollywood vs. America* (New York: HarperCollins, 1992), 191.

8. "Sexual Violence on Television," *U.S. News & World Report* 119, no. 10 (11 September 1995), 62.

9. David Walsh, *Selling Out America's Children: How America Puts Profits Before Values and What Parents Can Do* (Minneapolis: Fairview Press, 1994), 15.

10. *Washington Times*, as reported in the *AFA Journal*, (February, 1997), 4.

11. "The Web's Dirty Secret," *U.S. News & World Report 121, no. 7* (19 August 1996), 51.

Chapter 12: Sexual Problems

1. Roy Eskapa, as quoted in *Dictionary of Sex Quotations*, 238.

2. Alex Comfort, *A Good Age*, (New York: Simon and Schuster, 1976), 193.

Glossary

Abortion. The termination of pregnancy before birth. There are two types of abortion:

(1) **Spontaneous:** A naturally occurring end to the pregnancy; also called a miscarriage.

(2) **Elective:** An abortion which is the surgical or medical termination of a pregnancy.

Elective abortion procedures:

- **D & C (Dilation and Curettage).** A procedure used during the first 12 weeks of pregnancy in which the cervix is dilated and the uterine lining (including the baby) is scraped out by a loop-shaped instrument known as a curette.

- **D & E (Dilation and Evacuation).** A procedure where forceps are inserted into the womb to grasp the fetus and tear it apart until the remains can be suctioned out.

- **RU-486 (mifepristone).** An abortifacient drug that causes the uterus to expel the baby.

- **Saline and Prostaglandin.** A procedure in which saline is injected into the amniotic sac to kill the baby and, if needed, prostaglandin is given to induce contractions.

- **Vacuum Curettage.** A procedure in which, upon dilating the cervix, a loop-shaped knife (curette) is inserted into the uterus to cut the baby apart. The remains of the baby are suctioned out through a thin plastic tube.

Abstinence. To voluntarily refrain from sexual intercourse.

Acquaintance Rape (Date Rape). A rape where the perpetrator is known by the victim.

Acquired Immunodeficiency Syndrome (AIDS). A viral disease, usually fatal, which is transmitted through the exchange of body fluids; usually blood or semen.

Acrotomophilia. See Sexual Paraphilias.

Adoption. To take a child into one's family through legal means and raise the child as one's own.

Afterbirth. The tissues that are expelled after childbirth, including the placenta, the remains of the umbilical cord, and any other fetal membranes.

Agape. See Love.

AIDS. See Acquired Immunodeficiency Syndrome.

Alprostadil. A drug self-injected into the base of the penis to help produce an erection.

Altruistic Surrogacy. Surrogate motherhood done by a friend or a relative who is motivated by the desire to do good.

Amniocentesis. A test where the fetal cells in the amniotic fluid are tested for signs of birth defects, such as Down's syndrome.

Amnion. A thin membrane formed as a sac around the unborn baby.

Amniotic Fluid. The fluid contained in the amnion which protects and cushions the newly forming life from shocks and jolts.

Anal Sex. The insertion of the penis into a partner's rectum.

Anal/Oral Sex. Licking or insertion of the tongue into the partner's rectum. It is also called *rimming.*

Areola. The area surrounding the nipple of a woman's breast; it varies in size and color, though usually is much darker than the rest of the breast.

Artificial Insemination. See Infertility Treatments.

Asexual. A low interest in sex.

Autosomes. The 22 matching pairs of nonsex chromosomes which are formed by the 22 maternal and the 22 male chromosomes during fertilization.

Baby Boom. A period of history marked by a rapid rise in the birth rate, as in the U.S. from 1945 to 60 when couples were having an average of 3.7 children.

Barrier Methods. Forms of birth control that use objects to block the sperm from getting to the egg. Some of the more common barrier methods are (1) the diaphragm; (2) the cervical cap; (3) the male condom; (4) the female condom, and (5) foams, creams, gels, and sponges. See Birth Control.

Bartholin's Glands. Small glands and their ducts located just inside the minor lips in a female's genitalia that produce a small amount of secretion during sexual arousal.

Becoming One Flesh. A biblical word for intercourse, when two people are in relationship physically, emotionally, and spiritually.

Benign Prostatic Hypertrophy (BPH). Prostate enlargement.

Bestiality. The act of engaging in sex with animals.

Beta Blockers. Prescription medicines used to regulate the circulatory system; also used to make sex easier on the heart.

Biastophilia. See Sexual Paraphilias.

Birth Canal. The term used for the vagina during childbirth.

Birth Control. The control and prevention of conception or birth. There are many methods available including the following:

- **Abstinence.** When one refrains from intercourse. Refraining from intercourse during the fertile period of a woman's cycle is called natural family planning, or "the rhythm method."

- **Abortion.** Medical or surgical termination of pregnancy. See Abortion.

- **Cervical Cap.** A device that is much like the diaphragm, in that it also fits over the cervix; however, the cap is much smaller.

- **Condom (Female).** A pouch inserted into the vagina during sexual intercourse.

- **Condom (Male).** A soft, flexible sheath that is placed over the man's penis in order to block sperm from entering the vagina.

- **Depo-Provera.** Injection of a long-acting progestin every 12 weeks: creates an atmosphere hostile to the implantation of the embryo.

- **Diaphragm.** A latex rubber disk with a flexible rim that is placed into the vagina and over the cervix.

- **IUD (Intrauterine Device).** A small, plastic T-shaped device that is inserted into the uterus. It has a nylon thread attached to the end, which is left hanging into the vagina so that the woman can check to make sure the IUD is in place. There are presently two types available: (1) one called the Copper T, which is plastic with copper wound around it; (2) one called the progestasert, which releases a synthetic hormone called progestin.

- **Norplant.** An implant of small plastic tubes filled with levonorgestrel, a form of progestin, that are inserted just under the skin a woman's arm; effective for up to five years.

- **Pill (Female).** A pill, usually a combination of progestin and estrogen, taken to keep the ovaries from releasing eggs and/or to keep the embryo from implanting in the uterus.

- **Pill (Male).** A hormonal birth control method that is still in the research stage. A synthetic version of testosterone, the male hormone, would be used in order to stop the production of sperm.

- **Spermicides.** Sperm-killing chemicals that are added to creams, foams, jellies, and sponges.

- **Tubal Ligation.** Cutting and tying the fallopian tubes, thus preventing egg and sperm from meeting.

- **Vasectomy.** Cutting and tying the vas deferens, thus preventing sperm from leaving the man's body.

Bisexual. People who are sexually attracted to both genders.

Bondage. See Sadomasochism (S & M).

Breech Birth. The birth position in which the baby's feet or buttocks appear first, instead of the usual (head-first) position.

Celibate. State of being unmarried with no sex partner.

Cervical Cap. See Birth Control.

Cervix. The lower, narrowed part of the uterus.

Chancroid. An STD caused by a bacterium that manifests itself as a small pimple(s) on the genitals.

Change of Life. See Menopause.

Chlamydia. See Sexually Transmitted Diseases (STDs).

Circumcision (Female). See Clitoridectomy.

Circumcision (Male). The removal of the foreskin, the skin that covers the glans, the head of the penis, for religious and/or hygienic reasons.

Climacteric. See Menopause.

Climax. See Orgasm.

Clitoral Hood. See Labia Minora.

Clitoridectomy. Also called female circumcision, the surgical removal of the clitoris as well, at times, of some of the outer genital area.

Clitoris. The small female organ found in the vulva that corresponds to the male penis in its ability to become erect or extended when aroused.

Cloning. See Infertility Treatments.

Coitus. Sexual intercourse; insertion of the penis into the vagina.

Commercial Surrogacy. Surrogate motherhood done for a fee.

Communications Decency Act. Until struck down by the Supreme Court in June of 1997, the act that made it a crime to send or display indecent or obscene material over the Internet where it could be seen by children.

Conception. The penetration of the egg (ovum) by a sperm.

Condom (Female and Male). See Birth Control.

Constructive Force. Someone of a higher military rank taking advantage sexually of someone of lower rank.

Copper T. See Birth Control, IUD.

Corona. The raised ridge surrounding the head of the penis.

Cowper's Glands. Two glands in the male that produce a lubricant known as pre-ejaculation fluid.

Cross-Dressing. Dressing up in clothing that is worn by members of the opposite sex.

- **Drag Queens.** Men who dress in women's clothes.

- **Drag Kings.** Women who dress in men's clothes.

Cunnilingus. See Oral Sex.

Cybersex. Engaging in sex via the Internet.

Cytomegalovirus (CMV). An untreatable STD that can cause hearing loss and mental retardation when a newborn baby is affected due to the mother's infection.

D & C (Dilation and Curettage). See Abortion, Elective.

D & E (Dilation and Evacuation). See Abortion, Elective.

Dalkon Shield. An IUD commonly used in the 1970s, but because of complications with pelvic inflammatory disease, was removed from the market.

Date Rape. See Acquaintance Rape.

Delayed Ejaculation. See Sexual Dysfunctions (Male).

Delivery. The act of giving birth.

Depo-Provera. See Birth Control.

Diaphragm. See Birth Control.

DNA (Deoxyribonucleic Acid). The chemical in each cell where the genetic code is stored.

Donor Egg. See Infertility Treatments.

Douche. A stream of liquid or air applied to a part or cavity of the body for cleansing or medicinal purposes; specifically, a solution injected into the vagina.

Drag King. See Cross Dressing.

Drag Queen. See Cross Dressing.

Dyspareunia. See Sexual Dysfunction (Female).

Ectopic Pregnancy. Fetal development outside the uterus, usually in the fallopian tube.

Egg. See Ovum.

Ejaculation. The discharge of semen from the penis.

Elective Abortion. See Abortion.

Embryo. The unborn baby at its earliest stage of development—the first eight weeks of the growing, fertilized ovum.

Endometriosis. A major cause of infertility in which the endometrium grows out of the uterus into surrounding organs such as the abdominal cavity, on the ovaries, and/or the fallopian tubes.

Endometrium. The mucous membrane lining the uterus that thickens and fills with blood monthly in preparation for a fertilized ovum.

Epididymis. Tubules, directly on top of the testis, where sperm mature and prepare to leave the body.

Episiotomy. Surgical cutting of the vagina in order to prevent the baby from tearing the opening as it exits.

Erection. The enlargement and hardening of the penis or clitoris as tissues fill with blood, usually during sexual arousal.

Erogenous Zones. The areas of the body that are particularly sensitive to sexual stimulation, such as the genitals, nipples, breasts, lips, and mouth.

Eros. See Love.

Erotica. Thought of as different from pornography in that it presents nudity or sexual activity in an artistic way.

Eunuch. Someone whose testes are removed.

Exhibitionism. The act of exposing one's genitals to someone else for the sake of receiving sexual gratification.

Failure to Reach Orgasm. See Sexual Dysfunctions (Female).

Fallopian Tubes. The two tubes located close to the ovaries through which the egg passes from each ovary to the uterus.

Fellatio. See Oral Sex.

Female-on-Top Position. See Sexual Positions.

Fertility Drugs. See Infertility Treatments.

Fertilization. See Conception.

Fetal Tissue. Tissue from an aborted fetus, sometimes used in experimentation by researchers to help treat certain diseases.

Fetishism. Fixation of erotic interest on a part of the body, such as the foot, or an article of clothing, or other object.

Fetus. The unborn child from the third month after conception until birth.

Fimbria. Cilia or finger-like fringes at the ovary end of each fallopian tube that sweep the ovum into the tube after it is released by the ovary.

Follicle. The small sac near the surface of the ovary that holds the developing egg cell (ovum).

Foreskin. The loose skin that covers the glans, or tip, of the penis.

Fraternal Twins. Twins who are not alike (or identical) born as a result of two different eggs fertilized by two separate sperm.

Frenulum. The thin band of skin that runs the length of the underside of the penis.

Frigidity. See Sexual Dysfunctions (Female).

Frotteurism. See Sexual Paraphilias.

G Spot. A small area in the vagina, discovered by a German physician named Grafenberg, that is more sensitive during intercourse than the rest of the vaginal tissue.

Gamete Intrafallopian Transfer (GIFT). See Infertility Treatments.

Gay. Another word for a homosexual. See Homosexuality.

Gender. A classification determined by sex, either male or female.

Genetic Surrogacy. When a surrogate mother contributes the egg and the uterus and is artificially inseminated by the husband of the infertile couple.

Genital Herpes. See Sexually Transmitted Diseases (STDs).

Genital Warts. See Sexually Transmitted Diseases (STDs), Human Papilloma Virus (HPV).

Genitalia. The internal and external sex and reproductive organs in the man and woman. Also known as genitals and genital organs.

Gestational Surrogacy. When a surrogate mother contributes only the uterus, with the egg coming from the wife of the infertile couple after having been fertilized by the husband's sperm through in vitro fertilization.

Glans. The tip of the male penis as well as the female clitoris.

Gonorrhea. See Sexually Transmitted Diseases (STDs).

HIV. See Sexually Transmitted Diseases (STDs).

Homocidophilia. See Sexual Paraphilias.

Homophobia. The irrational fear and hatred of homosexuals, to the extent that one may want to even do physical harm to homosexuals.

Homophobic. A person who fears and hates homosexuals.

Homosexuality. Sexual orientation toward someone of the same sex. The names used to describe this same-sex orientation are *gay* for men and *lesbian* for women.

Human Immunodeficiency Virus (HIV). A virus that attacks the human immune system; see Sexually Transmitted Diseases (STDs).

Human Papilloma Virus (HPV). See Sexually Transmitted Diseases (STDs).

Hymen. A thin membrane of skin covering the opening of the vagina. It is also known as the maidenhead.

Hyperphilia. When one has sex more often than most people.

Hypophilia. When one never has sex or has it infrequently.

Hysterectomy. A surgical removal of the uterus and sometimes the fallopian tubes and ovaries.

Identical Twins. Twins who are of the same sex and look alike due to the result of one egg fertilized by one sperm and the egg then splitting into two.

Impotence. See Sexual Dysfunctions (Male).

Infertility. A diagnosis made when a healthy couple has not conceived after one year of sexual intercourse without the use of contraceptives of any kind.

Infertility Treatments. Treatments to help infertile couples have children. Here is a list of some of the treatments:

- **Artificial Insemination by Donor (AID).** A procedure in which sperm is taken from donors and then inserted into a woman's body.

- **Artificial Insemination by Husband (AIH).** A procedure in which sperm is taken from the husband, concentrated, and then inserted into his wife's body. In another procedure, called direct sperm injection, the husband's sperm is injected directly into an egg during IVF.

- **Cloning.** A procedure in which there is a transfer of the chromosomes from the body cell of an organism into an ovum from which all chromosomal material has been removed; the ovum develops into an exact genetic duplicate of the original body cell.

- **Donor Egg.** A procedure in which the eggs of a fertile woman are harvested and then used for fertilization through insertion into an infertile woman's uterus.

- **Fertility Drugs.** Drugs such as Metrodin and Clomid that are taken to help increase chances of the fertilization of the egg and the sperm.

- **Gamete Intrafallopian Transfer (GIFT).** A procedure in which the sperm and eggs are mixed outside the body and placed in the fallopian tubes to fertilize rather than in a sterile dish.

- **In Vitro Fertilization (IVF).** A procedure in which the eggs of the woman and the sperm of the man are put "in glass" for fertilization and then placed into the woman's uterus.

- **Surrogate Motherhood.** Placing a woman's developing embryo into another woman's uterus because the first woman cannot, or chooses not to, carry her own child.

• **Zygote Intrafallopian Transfer (ZIFT).** A procedure in which a woman's egg(s) are fertilized outside the body and then are reinserted into the woman's fallopian tubes.

In Vitro Fertilization (IVF). See Infertility Treatments.

Intercourse, Sexual. Sexual activity in which insertion of the penis occurs.

• **Anal Intercourse:** Insertion of the penis into another person's anus.

• **Oral Intercourse.** Insertion of the penis into a partner's mouth.

• **Vaginal Intercourse.** Insertion of the penis into the vagina; also known as coitus.

Intrauterine Device. See Birth Control.

IUD (Intrauterine Device). See Birth Control.

Kleptophilia. See Sexual Paraphilias.

Klismaphilia. See Sexual Paraphilia.

Labia Majora (The Major Lips). The two folds between the woman's legs that cover the minor lips, clitoris, urethral opening, and vaginal opening.

Labia Minora (The Minor Lips). The two parallel folds of skin that connect as a hood over the clitoris.

Labor. The birth stage in which the cervix gradually dilates, allowing strong contractions of the uterine muscles to push the baby through the vagina and out of the mother's body.

Lactation. The process by which the clusters of milk glands in the breasts begin the production of milk at the birth of a child.

Lamaze. A birth technique named after French doctor Fernand Lamaze, in which a series of breathing exercises are used during the different stages of labor to help ease the pain of childbirth.

Lanugo. The furry hair that covers the baby in the womb after the first six months.

Lateral Position. See Sexual Positions, Side-by-Side.

Lesbian. A female homosexual.

Levonorgestrel. A form of progestin that is placed in small plastic tubes and inserted into a woman's arm to prevent ova from being released (Norplant).

Love. Strong feelings expressing everything from deep sexual desire and passion to affection and friendship. Four kinds of love can be distinguished:

- **Agape.** A love that is totally unselfish and has the capacity to give and keep on giving without expecting a return.

- **Eros.** A love that is erotic, romantic, and passionate.

- **Philia.** A friendship love characterized by a sharing of thoughts and feelings.

- **Romantic Love.** A love that encompasses agape, eros, philia and storge love. Though romantic love can exist without all four aspects of love being present, most married couples experience their greatest satisfaction when each one is functioning well.

- **Storge.** A natural affection for another person that expresses security and acceptance.

Maidenhead. See Hymen.

Major Lips. See Labia Majora.

Male-Behind Position. See Sexual Positions.

Male-on-Top Position. See Sexual Positions.

Mammogram. A sensitive X-ray procedure used to discover small breast tumors.

Marital Rape. Forced sex in marriage.

Masturbation. Stimulation of the genital organs, usually to orgasm, by means other than sexual intercourse.

Meatus. The opening at the end of the penis through which urine and sperm pass.

Menarche. The first time of menstruation, beginning around ages 9 to 16.

Menopause. The period of cessation of menstruation, occurring usually between the ages of 45 and 52. Also known as "change of life" and "climacteric."

Menstrual Cycle. The hormonal interactions within a woman that prepare the body for possible pregnancy.

Menstruation. The time of the menstrual cycle, also called the period, when the inner uterine lining and other dead blood cells are discharged through the vagina.

Minor Lips. See Labia Minora.

Miscarriage. See Abortion, Spontaneous.

Missionary Position. See Sexual Positions.

Mons Pubis. The most visible part of the woman's genitals, the fatty tissue above the sex organs on the pubic bone. At puberty, hair grows and covers most of this area.

Morning-after Pill. A drug given to a woman the day after unprotected intercourse to discourage a fertilized ovum from implanting in the uterus.

Mutual Masturbation. Partners stimulating each other to orgasm.

Mysophilia. See Sexual Paraphilia.

Narratophilia. See Sexual Paraphilia.

Natural Family Planning. See Birth Control.

Necrophilia. See Sexual Paraphilia.

Norplant. See Birth Control.

Nymphomania. Excessive sexual drive experienced by a woman in which she is unable to control her sexual behavior even though it may mean serious consequences.

Obscenity. Utterances, gestures, and the like that are offensive to public taste and morals.

Oceanic Position. See Sexual Positions.

Oral Intercourse. See Intercourse, Sexual.

Oral Sex. Oral stimulation of another person's genitalia.

- **Cunnilingus:** Licking or sucking the woman's vulva area, especially her clitoris.

- **Fellatio:** Licking or sucking the penis.

Orgasm. A series of rhythmic contractions brought about by physical and psychological stimulation, also known as the climax.

Outercourse. Expressing love in ways other than through penile penetration, such as stroking and touching each other's bodies.

Ovaries. The two female sex glands found on either side of the uterus in which the ova (egg cells) are formed and hormones are produced that influence female body characteristics.

Ovulation. Release of the mature (ripe) ovum from the ovary to the fallopian tubes.

Ovum. Human egg cell produced by female ovaries (plural: ova).

Paraphilias. See Sexual Paraphilias.

Pedophile. One who engages in sexual activity with children.

Pedophilia. The use of children as the object of sexual gratification.

Peeping Tom. Someone who is sexually aroused at viewing others who are engaged in a sexual act or who are nude.

Pelvic Inflammatory Disease. See Sexually Transmitted Diseases (STDs).

Penis. The male sex organ through which semen is released and urine is expelled.

Perineum. The area between the anus and genitalia.

Philia. See Love.

Pictophilia. See Sexual Paraphilia.

PID. See Sexually Transmitted Diseases (STDs), Pelvic Inflammatory Disease.

Pill (Female and Male). See Birth Control.

Placenta. The sponge-like organ that connects the fetus to the lining of the uterus by means of the umbilical cord. It serves to provide nourishment and remove waste from the developing baby. It is expelled from the uterus after the birth a child (afterbirth).

Pornography. Literature, motion pictures, art, or other means of expression that, without any concern for personal or moral values, intend simply to be sexually arousing.

Pregnancy. The period from conception to birth; the condition of having a developing embryo or fetus within the female body.

Premature Ejaculation. See Sexual Dysfunction (Male).

Premenstrual Syndrome (PMS). Physical and emotional difficulties experienced by some women during the week prior to their menstrual period. Symptoms include abdominal bloating, tender breasts, irritability, and mood swings.

Prenatal Care. Medical observation and care given to the mother and unborn baby prior to birth.

Prepuce. A hood covering the tip of the clitoral glans; the loose skin covering the tip of the penis, removed during circumcision.

Priapism. See Sexual Dysfunctions (Male).

Progestasert. See Birth Control, IUD.

Progestin. A synthetic duplication of the female hormone progesterone, which changes the chemical makeup of the cervical mucus, preventing sperm from easily passing into the uterus, and creates an atmosphere in the uterine lining that makes it difficult for implantation of a fertilized egg.

Prostaglandin Abortion. See Abortion, Elective.

Prostate. A gland in the male that is located beneath the urinary bladder and produces some of the substances of semen.

Prostate-Specific Antigen (PSA). A blood test that determines the possibility of prostate cancer.

Pyromania. See Sexual Paraphilia.

Rape. Forcing sexual intercourse with a person who does not consent.

Retarded Ejaculation. See Sexual Dysfunctions (Male).

Rhythm Method. A natural method of birth control that is determined by a woman's menstrual-fertility cycle.

Rimming. See Anal/Oral Sex.

Romantic Love. See Love.

RU-486 (mifepristone). See Abortion, Elective.

Sadomasochism (S & M). The application of pain or humiliation for the sake of sexual gratification, also known as bondage.

Saline Abortion. See Abortion, Elective.

Saliromania. See Sexual Paraphilia.

Satyriasis. Excessive sexual desire experienced by a man, so intense that he is unable to control his behavior even though it may mean serious consequences.

Saline Abortion. See Abortion, Elective.

Scrotum. The sac of skin that hangs between the legs of a male and encloses the testes (testicles).

Semen. A milky, sticky fluid made up of sperm and secretions from the seminal vesicles, prostate, Cowper's glands, and the epididymis. Ejaculated through the penis when the male reaches orgasm.

Seminal Vesicles. Glands at the end of the vas deferens in which seminal fluid is produced.

Sexual Addiction. A misdirected sex drive that goes beyond the biological need to have closeness, sexual release, or to reproduce.

Sexual Dysfunction. Any difficulty with sex and the sex act such as impotence, frigidity, premature ejaculation, or trouble reaching an orgasm.

Sexual Dysfunctions (Female). Problems in sexual performance, including the following:

- **Dyspareunia.** Painful intercourse, closely related to vaginismus.

- **Failure to Reach Orgasm.** Inability to climax sexually.

- **Frigidity.** When a woman shows little, if any, desire for sex.

- **Vaginismus.** An involuntary spasm of the muscles within the vagina that makes intercourse painful and often impossible.

Sexual Dysfunctions (Male). Problems in sexual performance, including the following:

- **Impotence.** Difficulty getting or maintaining an erection.

- **Premature Ejaculation.** Ejaculation that occurs before a man wants it to occur.

- **Priapism.** A permanent erection.

- **Retarded (or Delayed) Ejaculation.** Inability to ejaculate even though an erection is maintained.

Sexual Intercourse. See Intercourse, Sexual.

Sexual Paraphilia. Sexual attraction to an object or to a situation that is not considered a normal way of becoming sexually aroused. These are some of the less common paraphilia:

- **Acrotomophilia.** Arousal from imagining oneself as a amputee.

- **Asphyxophilia.** Arousal from strangulating (cutting intake of oxygen) oneself.

- **Biastophilia.** Arousal from sexually attacking someone unexpectedly.

- **Frotteurism.** Arousal from anonymously pressing or rubbing one's genitals against another, usually in a public, crowded place.

- **Homocidophilia.** Arousal from thinking about murdering one's partner.

- **Kleptophilia.** Arousal from stealing.

- **Klismaphilia.** Arousal from taking enemas.

- **Mysophilia.** Arousal from soiled underwear.

- **Narratophilia.** Arousal from erotic narratives.

- **Necrophilia.** Arousal from sex with a dead person.

- **Pictophilia.** Arousal from viewing pornography.

- **Pyromania.** Arousal from firesetting.

- **Saliromania.** Arousal from damaging or soiling the body or clothing of a woman.

- **Transvestophilia.** Arousal from wearing clothing, such as underwear, of the opposite sex.

Sexual Orientation. Refers to the gender a person is emotionally and physically attracted to.

Sexual Positions. The positions in which a couple arrange themselves during sexual intercourse.

- **Female-on-Top Position.** In this position, the man lies on his back and the woman tilts forward and moves her vagina onto his penis.

- **Male-Behind Position.** Also known as the "spoon position", in which both partners lie in the same direction, with the man straddling up close behind his wife, allowing him to enter her vagina from behind.

- **Missionary Position.** A face-to-face position, also known as the male-on-top position.

- **Side-by-Side Position.** Also known as the lateral position, in which the partners lie next to one another, facing while having sexual intercourse.

- **Squatting Position.** Also known as the oceanic position, in which the woman lies down and spreads her legs as the man squats over her and thrusts his penis into her vagina.

- **Standing-Up Position.** The man, standing, picks up the woman, and, as she wraps her legs around his body, thrusts his penis into her vagina.

Sexually Transmitted Diseases (STDs). Diseases that are generally spread through sexual intercourse. Here is a list of some of the primary STDs:

- **Chlamydia.** Caused by a minute parasite that invades the cells, multiplying within them, and causing urethritis in males and often no symptoms in females. May lead to sterility.

- **Genital Herpes.** A viral STD that causes painful sores on the sexual organs.

- **Gonorrhea.** A bacterial STD that can cause burning and itching in the urethra as well as sterility in the female.

- **HIV.** The human immunodeficiency virus; it attacks the immune system, eventually causing AIDS.

- **Human Papilloma Virus (HPV).** A viral STD, also known as genital warts, that causes lesions and can even lead to cancerous malignancies.

- **Pelvic Inflammatory Disease (PID).** An STD (can be caused by either gonorrhea or chlamydia) that spreads into a woman's reproductive organs, causing sterility and great pain.

- **Syphilis.** A bacterial STD that goes through a series of stages, often beginning with a chancre.

Shaft. The cylindrical main part of the penis.

Side-by-Side Position. See Sexual Positions.

Sodomy. Any of a variety of sexual behaviors, broadly defined by law as deviant, such as sexual intercourse by humans with animals or anal intercourse between human beings.

Sperm. The male reproductive cell(s), produced in the testicles, having the capacity to fertilize the female ova, resulting in pregnancy.

Spermicides. See Birth Control.

Spontaneous Abortion. See Abortion.

Spoon Position. See Sexual Positions.

Squatting Position. See Sexual Positions.

Squeeze Technique. A technique used for curing premature ejaculation, in which the husband or wife squeezes or pinches for several seconds the erect penis where the glans joins the shaft, decreasing the flow of blood and causing the man to lose part of his erection.

Standing-Up Position. See Sexual Positions.

Sterilization. A surgical procedure to prevent pregnancy.

Storge. See Love.

Surfactant. A substance produced by a layer of cells that line the air sacs within the lungs and that keeps the newborn's lungs from collapsing after birth.

Surrogate Motherhood. See Infertility Treatments.

Syphilis. See Sexually Transmitted Diseases (STDs).

Telephone Scatologia. Obscene telephone calls.

Telephone Sex. Sexually provocative phone conversation, usually for pay.

Testes. See Testicles.

Testicles. The two male sex glands, also known as testes (singular: testis), that produce sperm and androgens, which are the steroid hormones (testosterone) that develop and maintain masculine characteristics (as estrogen does for females).

Testosterone. The male sex hormone.

Tongue Bathing. When a couple use their tongues to lick and kiss each other all over.

Transvestites. Those who cross-dress for sexual gratification.

Transvestophilia. See Sexual Paraphilia.

Transsexuals. People who fully identify with the opposite gender through dress and who inwardly desire to be that gender biologically as well.

Trichomonoas. A vaginal infection, also known as trich.

Tubal Ligation. See Birth Control.

Urethra. The duct through which urine passes from the bladder and is eliminated from the body. In men, this duct also serves to transmit semen through the penis to the woman's vagina and uterus.

Urinary Tract Infection (UTI). An infection caused by a bacterium usually transmitted from the rectum to either the penis or the vagina.

Uterus. The muscular, pear-shaped female organ, also known as the womb, in which the fetus develops.

Vacuum Curettage. See Abortion, Elective.

Vagina. The passage between the uterus and the vulva that receives the penis during intercourse and through which the baby passes during birth.

Vaginal/Oral Sex. Licking or inserting the tongue into the partner's vagina.

Vaginismus. See Sexual Dysfunction (Female).

Vas Deferens. The long slender tube that carries sperm from the epididymis into the body cavity and to the seminal vesicles.

Vasectomy. See Birth Control.

Vernix. A protective ointment that is secreted from special glands surrounding the hair follicles of the growing fetus within the mother's womb.

Viagra. An impotency pill, introduced in 1998, used to prolong the effects of cyclic GMP, the chemical that causes the muscles in the penis to relax and the arteries to expand.

Virgin. Someone who has not had sexual intercourse.

Voyeurism. Sexual gratification from viewing others who are engaged in a sexual act or who are nude.

Vulva. The external female genitalia or sex organs, including the mons pubis, major and minor lips, clitoris, and the opening into the vagina.

Womb. See Uterus.

X Chromosome. A chromosome that determines gender, present in all female ova and in one-half of all male sperm.

Y Chromosome. A sex-determining chromosome present in one-half of all male sperm, but not in the female ova.

Zygote. A newly fertilized egg, or the single cell that results from the union of the sperm and egg at conception.

Zygote Intrafallopian Transfer (ZIFT). See Infertility Treatments.

About the author

Roger Sonnenberg holds a Master of Divinity degree from Concordia Seminary in St. Louis, MO, as well as a master's degree in psychotherapy from The American Institute of Family Relations in Los Angeles, CA. He pastors a large church in Arcadia, CA. He serves as a part-time professor in the graduate marriage and family program at Concordia University, Seward, NE. Roger also lectures and conducts seminars throughout the United States on sexuality, family, and marriage. He is the author of many articles, studies, and books, including *Parenting with Purpose* and *Parenting with Values*, two video-based parenting programs (Family Films, St. Louis, MO), plus two recent books, *501 Practical Ways to Love Your Wife & Kids* and *501 Ways to Love Your Grandkids & and Their Parents* (CPH, St. Louis, MO).